Lord, Why?

Lord, Why?

*Questioning God
When Life Hurts*

Sanford Zensen

WIPF & STOCK · Eugene, Oregon

Lord, Why?

Questioning God When Life Hurts

by

Sanford Zensen

WIPF & STOCK . Eugene, Oregon

Copyright © 2024

Softcover ISBN: 979-8-3852-1055-8
Hardcover ISBN: 979-8-3852-1056-5
eBook ISBN: 979-8-3852-1057-2

All rights reserved. Except for brief quotations in critical publications or reviews, no part of this book may be reproduced in any manner without prior written permission from the publisher.

Write: Permissions, Wipf and Stock Publishers
199 W. 8th Ave, Suite 3, Eugene, OR 97401

Unless otherwise noted Scripture quotations are taken from the *New American Standard Bible®* (NASB), Copyright © 1960, 1962, 1963, 1968, 1971, 1972, 1973,1975, 1977, 1995 by The Lockman Foundation. Used by permission. www.Lockman.org.

Scriptures quotations marked (AVS are taken from the *American Standard Version* (1901), Public Domain.

Scripture quotations marked (AMP) are taken from the *Amplified® Bible*, Copyright © 2015 by The Lockman Foundation. Used by permission. www.Lockman.org.

Scripture quotations marked (AMPC) are taken from the *Amplified Bible, Classic Education,* Copyright © 1965 2015 by The Lockman Foundation. Used by permission. www.Lockman.org.

Scripture quotations marked (ESV) are from *The Holy Bible, English Standard Version®* (ESV®), copyright © 2001 by Crossway, a publishing ministry of Good News Publishers. Used by permission. All rights reserved.

Scriptures marked (KJV) are taken from the *King James Version*, public domain.

Scripture quotations marked (MSG) are taken from *The Message*, copyright © 1993, 1994, 1995, 1996, 2000, 2001, 2002 by Eugene H. Peterson. Used by permission of NavPress. All rights reserved. Represented by Tyndale House Publishers, Inc.

Scripture marked (NKJV) taken from the *New King James Version*®. Copyright © 1982 by Thomas Nelson. Used by permission.

Scripture quotations marked (NIV) are taken from the Holy Bible, *New International Version*®, NIV®. Copyright © 1973, 1978, 1984, 2011 by Biblica, Inc.™ Used by permission of Zondervan. All rights reserved worldwide. www.zondervan.com The "NIV" and "New International Version" are trademarks registered in the United States Patent and Trademark Office by Biblica, Inc.™

Scripture quotations marked (NLT) are taken from the Holy Bible, *New Living Translation* Copyright © 1996, 2004, 2007 by Tyndale House Foundation. Used by permission of Tyndale House Publishers Inc., Carol Stream, IL 60188. All rights reserved. New Living, NLT, and the New Living Translation logo are registered trademarks of Tyndale House Publishers.

Scripture quotations marked (PHILLIPS) are taken from *The New Testament in Modern English*, copyright 1958, 1959, 1960 J.B. Phillips and 1947, 1952, 1955, 1957, 1976, The MacMillan Company, New York. Used by permission. All rights reserved.

Scripture quotations marked (TPT) are from *The Passion Translation*®. Copyright © 2017, 2018 by Passion & Fire Ministries, Inc. Used by permission. All rights reserved. ThePassionTranslation.com.

Scripture quotations marked (ASV) are taken from *American Standard Version*, Public domain.

Bracketed [ ] comments in Scripture and quotes are the author's.

Lord, I ask more questions
Than You ask.
The ratio, I would suppose,
Is ten to one.
I ask:
Why do You permit this anguish?
How long can I endure it?
What possible purpose does it serve?
Have You forgotten to be gracious?
Have I wearied You?
Have I offended You?
Have You cast me off?
Where did I miss Your guidance?
When did I lose the way?
Do You see my utter despair?
You ask:
Are you trusting Me?[1]
–Ruth Harms Calkin

At first, it seems a little thing,
A want unmet, a prayer unwinged.
Voiceless, it interrogates the King,
When sounded, Lucifer sings.[2]
–Greg Morse, *Desiring God*

---

[1] Ruth Harms Calkin, Too Many Questions, *My Diaries*, October 10, 2010, retrieved from https://www.my-diary.org/read/e/321389/troysoon%3A-too-many-questions.

[2] Greg Morse, The Curse Under Our Breath: What Grumbling Sounds Like to God, Desiring God, January 8, 2023, retrieved from https://www.desiringgod.org/articles/the-curse-under-our-breath.

Acknowledgements

To my friend and fellow participant and servant in the Gospel of Jesus, Robert Day, a faithful man of God who has known his fair share of adversity over the years and has remained faithful to the call of God and the cause of Christ. My gratitude for the time and energy he invested in this book, for your constant encouragement, and the feedback you gave me throughout its writing that kept me honest and real, and focused on God's love, God's Word, and God's people. May the Lord bless you and keep you these days. May the great Shepherd of the sheep strengthen you and grant you much joy and peace in the Spirit until the moment you step through the gates of heaven and see the nail-scarred hands of your Savior, Christ Jesus, the Lamb of God. What a day of rejoicing that will be!

Contents

Introduction: Making Sense of It All 1

Chapter 1: God, Where Were You When I Needed You? 17

Chapter 2: Don't You Care? Why Don't You love me? 35

Chapter 3: Why So Much Pain and Suffering in the World? 47

Chapter 4: How Is This Helping Me? What Purpose Does All This Pain Serve? 65

Chapter 5: How Could You Let This Happen? 77

Chapter 6: When Are You Going to Call the Dogs Off? 93

Chapter 7: What Have I Done to Deserve This? 109

Conclusion: The Healing Balm 123

About the Author 131

> Life is hard. Then you die. Then they throw dirt in your face. Then the worms eat you. Be grateful it happens in that order.[3]
>
> –David Gerrold (American author)

INTRODUCTION

Making Sense of It All

Thomas V. Morris, a professor of philosophy at the University of Notre Dame, wrote in his book, *Making Sense of it All*:

> When you stop to think about it, life can be very confusing (an understatement if I ever read one)...you have no idea where you came from, how you got here, where in the world you are, or where you're going. You have no map or compass...For the most part, we sleepwalk through life. When something does happen to awaken us from our slumber, we sit befuddled, disoriented, perplexed.[4]

Daniel Hill worked at Starbucks. He was also on staff at Willow Creek Community Church, a mega-church located in the suburbs of Chicago. Daniel served in Axis, a program targeting a group of offbeat, unconventional, young people, who loved purple

---

[3] Staff Reports, Life is hard … grace is sufficient, *The Tribune*, February 20, 2020, retrieved from https://tribtown.com/2020/02/20/life_is_hard__grace_is_sufficient/.
[4] Thomas V. Morris, *Making Sense of it All*, (Grand Rapids, Michigan: Eerdmans, 1992), 1.

hair, belly-button rings, tattoos, and black-painted fingernails. They need Jesus, too.

The manager informed a new employee of Daniel's other job, the one working at Willow Creek. Wounded and scarred by a difficult, painful past, the woman became furious and anxious. She complained bitterly, "Three years ago my 16-year-old daughter was raped and murdered. Tell me, what kind of God would let that happen? I believe in God. I just have a real problem with Him."[5] So have I, especially when my faith has been tried and tested in the fires of adversity. Been there and done that.

Indeed, we are a bewildered people, living lives trying to understand troublesome events as they unfold before us each day. Life happens, and when it does, things can go terribly wrong very quickly, leaving us with few viable, satisfying answers to the great issues of life, death, and eternity. The harsh reality of living in a chaotic, often cruel and "confusing" world is depressing to say the least, especially when horrible experiences are displayed before our very eyes.

At times, it seems that life simply unravels, and we find ourselves unprepared for the onslaught of grief, overwhelming fear, and persistent doubts about the very existence of God, His faithfulness, and His power to make a difference in our daily lives. Everyday life is troublesome, and evil seems to march ahead unchecked. Apart from God, the future looks gloomy and dark indeed. Deep hurt and unimaginable pain and suffering abound everywhere, cutting across all socioeconomic levels, including generational, historical, and national boundaries. The world at large is not such a nice place. There is a plethora of seemingly "meaningless—totally senseless, or utterly pointless"[6] experiences common (in one form or another) to all men and women

---

[5] Brett Lawrence, Starbucks Spirituality, *Leadership,* Fall 2022, retrieved from http://www.christianitytoday.com/le/2002/fall/11.81.html

[6] *Op.cite*, Morris, 55

everywhere. If you have ever felt this way, you are not alone. Author and theologian, Friedrich Von Hugel (1852–1925) noted, *"The deeper we get into reality, the more numerous will be the questions we cannot answer."* Maybe he was on to something.

Kids are brutally honest and authentic. They have a way of finding mudholes and jumping in. They have questions and plenty of them. Here are a few directed at God in letters they have penned themselves. They are quite revealing.

KIDS' LETTERS TO GOD

- Do you throw lightning down at us? It scares me a lot when it goes BOOM. Please stop it!
- Why did You make snakes and spiders? I'm afraid of them.
- My teacher is mean. She always yells at us. She's old and ugly. Why did You make bad and mean people?
- My grandma is dying. She says You want her back with You, but I want her to stay here with me. You can have anyone You want. She's all I have, so please let her get better and stay.
- I play worse than anyone on my soccer team. I'm the smallest one, too. That doesn't seem very fair. Did You play a dirty trick on me?
- I hate it when Daddy drinks his beer. He smells awful. He gets mean and yells at me a lot. Did You make up beer? Why?
- God, do You ever cry? Who comforts You when you do?

Some years back, *Parade Magazine* asked celebrities, *"Knowing what you know now, what would you tell your younger self?"* Kiefer Sutherland said it best, "I'd tell myself, don't forget to duck.'" Good point. Life will eventually hit you up the side of the head and blind side you. You had better be prepared. Trouble is coming, which raises a lot of questions.

I've often said (with a smile). "I was a lot smarter, when I was younger." Older folk know what I'm talking about. I knew it all back then—or so I thought. I had an answer for everything. I was "brilliant," as I recall. What has happened since then? I can tell you…life happened, reality set in, experiences, disappointments, discouragements, and all the rest found me. Today, I have more questions than I do answers. Apparently, I'm not as smart as I once thought.

I once knew a vibrant, young, happily married mother of three small children who knew God and loved His Word. Her name was Anita. A family member informed me years later that Anita had memorized the entire chapter of Romans eight, focusing particularly on verse 28: *"And we know [with great confidence] that God [who is deeply concerned about us] causes all things to work together [as a plan] for good for those who love God, to those who are called according to His plan and purpose"* (Romans 8:28, AMP). She read those words. Believed those words. Lived those words. She was diagnosed not long later with an aggressive form of multiple sclerosis. The disease quickly destroyed her mind, ravaged her body, and eventually destroyed her marriage, her home, and her family. It was one of the saddest things I have ever witnessed. With blinding speed, Anita's emotional and mental state deteriorated to the level of a small child, needing 24/7 care. She was finally institutionalized for the remainder of her life, a terrible disease that robbed her of motherhood and her future. Consequently, her husband was forced to do what he never wanted or intended to do: divorce his wife to qualify her for state medical assistance. There was no other choice. They simply could not afford the ongoing medical care she so desperately needed. She died some years later, the shell of the woman who once loved life and loved her family.

From a human perspective, it seemed to be a useless, arbitrary event devoid of purpose and significant meaning. At least, that was how the family and I saw it at the time. Nothing about this tragedy made sense. The questions persisted and no one, including me, had answers. Where was God when this debilitating disease struck and ravaged a young couple and destroyed their futures? What possible reason could be offered? What was to be gained by it all? To what end? To this day, I remain in the dark, baffled and perplexed by the senseless loss of human dignity and life. The answers, I'm suspect, are locked away in the vaults of heaven, not to be revealed until eternity opens its gates once and for all. Professor Morris was right. Humanity remains "befuddled, disoriented, (and) perplexed."

In every situation of chaos and terror, wounded souls scream in agony, trying to make sense of daily life, trying to find answers for what has gone horribly wrong. In her devotional, *Daily Splashes of Joy*, Barbara Johnson suggested, "Pain maybe inevitable, but misery is optional."[7] She has a point. The search for understanding and solutions to what troubles us the most is real and consistent, and it often begins with the audacity of interrogating the King, Who by the way is God, the God Who invites us to *"taste and see that the Lord is good"* (Psalm 34:8, NIV). Such an invitation seems contradictory. The taste of some affairs and events in life seem bitter, and it burns like hot sauce poured over scrambled eggs.

I've heard it said (and have said it myself) many times that "God has our best interest at heart," that "God loves people more than anything else in the world," and that "God has a wonderful plan for your life." If you ask me, He has a "funny" way of showing it. Frankly, though all those statements may be true, it's still a rather bitter pill to swallow and harder to accept as "gospel truth," especially given the turmoil many people are forced to live with each

---

[7] Barbara Johnson, *Daily Splashes of Joy*, (Nashville, TN: W Publishing Group, 2000), 211.

day. Obviously, I choose to be miserable. I have chosen to "stain the honor of God" with my words.[8]

Like most, I have lots of questions leveled directly at God. In some respects, I have held Him personally responsible and accountable (at least temporarily) for what has or has not transpired in my daily life and in the lives of others I've personally known over the years. Flesh and blood assume that if there is a God in the universe (and there is), Who is as big and powerful, loving and kind as we think and say He is, then it stands to reason that He is fully capable of stepping into our lives, if He so chooses, and mercifully putting a stop to our misery and agony. At the very least, I expect God to effectively run interference on my behalf in a world fraught with roadblocks, potholes, and detours.

Under the stress of war and botched battles, Gideon felt abandoned by God. Anxious, discouraged, and fearful, he complained bitterly, *"If the Lord is with us* [as I had been told], *why then has all this happened to us* [me]? *And where are all His miracles which our fathers told us about?"* (Judges 6:13). A fair enough question I've asked on more than one occasion. I want…no, I demand answers from God. I insist on interrogating the King, Who has made the earth His footstool (Isaiah 66:1). My notion is ridiculous. Nevertheless, I still want to know what and why He has decreed and so ordered the affairs of my life, especially those not to my liking, which is, by the way, quite often.

Just hours after the University of Georgia football team celebrated its 2023 national championship victory over Texas Christian University, disaster struck. A player (offensive lineman, Devin Willock) and a recruiting staffer (Chandler LeCroy) were both killed in a car wreck. The vehicle was speeding and couldn't

---

[8] Charles Spurgeon, A Jealous God," *Metropolitan Tabernacle Pulpit Volume 9,* March 29, 1863, retrieved from https://www.spurgeon.org/resource-library/sermons/a-jealous-god/#flipbook/.

hold the road.⁹ There are no explanations worthy of consideration. Though there was evidence of alcohol, nothing could be said that would mend a broken heart and soften the blow of parents burying their son and daughter for whatever reason. This is the second such loss for Devin's father, whose oldest son also died in a car wreck a few years prior to Devin's death that fateful night. Did not God show up for the celebration following the game? Was He not in that car that plowed into a tree? Could He have stopped the incident? The answer is yes, yes, and yes. Instead, we got the bodies of two young people whose futures were no more. We have questions for the Almighty.

At first, we try a desperate plea for help from the only Source we know able to effectively halt any crisis we face and bring change, healing, and hope, settling the heart and mind in a time of great need (Philippians 4:7). The gatekeepers at the tabernacle of the Lord (1 Chronicles 9:19) saw God as their *"refuge and strength, always ready to help in times of trouble"* (Psalm 46:1, NLT). Stick with Him long enough, and you will find Him to be just that and more, *A Shelter in a Time of Storm*.¹⁰ However, for many others, God is blamed and found guilty of divine negligence in the courts of human opinion when trouble strikes. Well before all the "evidence" and facts are in, the verdict is read. God is guilty as charged.

God could have prevented the tragedy and the heartbreak but chose not to interfere for some unknown reason beyond our knowledge. So goes the reasoning, or should I dare say the complaints. Ultimately, we find God at fault for everything that has gone wrong. Rare is the man or woman who remembers God when things go well. Rather, we stand defiantly to point an accusing finger

---

⁹ Isabel Rosales, Jaide Timm-Garcia and Ryan Young, Police report says driver was speeding in crash that killed University of Georgia football player and staffer, *CNN*, January 17, 2023, retrieved from https://www.cnn.com/2023/01/17/us/uga-football-willock-lecroy-car-crash-tuesday/index.html.

¹⁰ Hymn title, composed by Vernon J. Charlesworth and sung by Ira Sankey, a contemporary of D.L. Moody.

heavenward, angry, fearful, confused, murmuring, and mumbling about God. Greg Morse, staff writer, for DesiringGod.org defined grumbling at God like this:

What is in a grumble? The sound, unheard in heaven, is the heart shaking its head, rolling its eyes, cursing under its breath. It is the seemingly harmless exhalation of several respectable sins — ingratitude, thanklessness, discontent. It's a controlled rage, an itchy contempt, the muffled echo of Satan's dismay. A broken tune. It can be voiced in a sigh or strangle a praise. It is the cough of a sick heart....a muffled mutiny.[11]

I have done considerable damage grumbling and complaining over the years, shamefully opening my disapproving, know-it-all mouth, only to insert my spiritual foot between my snarling lips. By the way, you can readily tell the size of my foot by the shape of my mouth. *"Who are you, O man (or woman), who answers back to God?"* asked the Apostle Paul (Romans 9:20). The answer to that question is the crux of the problem – arrogance, disbelief, brokenness. Let me take my foot from my mouth before I render a response.

I suspect that the real, down-to-earth answers for which we have no specific, immediate understanding are tucked away in the purposes of God somewhere in eternity past, present, and future. Someday, the mysteries of God will be revealed. For now, we had better learn to live with ambiguity until we are finally able to enter the pearly gates and catch a glimpse of who God really is and what He is about, which is the releasing of His power and the exercising of His will and wisdom throughout our lifetime and beyond. I firmly believe that God is able to bring "good" out of the most horrendous of circumstances and the chaos that envelopes everyday living, but will He, and when? That is the "million-dollar question." In the meantime, we struggle to make sense of our daily experiences. We know only this: God can redeem any situation we may find

---

[11] *Op.cite.*, Morse.

ourselves in (no matter how bad or hopeless it may seem) and deliver His best to your life and mine.

I am convinced that God is big enough to handle my inquiries (more like my inquisition) and gracious enough to let me rant and rave, complain and criticize, shout and scream, or wallow (at least for a while) in self-pity and doubts. I for one am glad that *"He knows (my) [mortal] frame; He remembers that I am [merely] dust"* (Psalm 103:14, AMP) and that I am limited in my comprehension and short on faith…in face, very short on both counts. There are times when I just need to put my big boy pants on and quit whining.

A number of years ago, I was teaching a college freshman level introduction to the Bible course. We were discussing the consequences of sin and the reality of life in a fallen world. I said to the class, "Plain and simple, sometimes life just stinks. In the language of today, 'Life just sucks.' Sometimes it is indescribably painful, excruciating, shockingly miserable, horrific, agonizingly intolerable."

A student approached me after class and angrily asked, "How could you say that? I am offended and aggravated. I'm disappointed that you would say such a thing. How could you talk about life like that? Where is your faith?"

I immediately wondered what planet the kid lived on, and then I replied, "I can say that because life sometime stinks. Some might say it just plain sucks! I can't say it any plainer than that. If you saw what I've seen, and been where I've been, and felt what I've felt, you might say the same thing. You are eighteen years old with little life experience, a college freshman. Come back and see me in twenty or thirty years and we will talk again."

He didn't thank me for my insights or for my response but stomped off outraged and disillusioned.

I can recall the words of a chorus I sang in Sunday school many years ago: "Ain't it grand to be a Christian, ain't it grand? Monday, Tuesday, Wednesday., etc….ain't it grand to be a

Christian?" Can you imagine the Christians of the first century being led into the arena to be torn apart by wild beasts, or watching their children, wives, husbands, and friends sawed in two for the sake of their faith and the cause of Christ, singing, "Ain't it grand to be a Christian, ain't it grand?" I think not.

I've thought about that over the years and have observed the life of the typical Christian living in the modern world or living in the jungles of Peru, or on the boarders of Israel facing the terror of Hamas, and trying to stay alive in a hostile environment. Trying to live life in a mixed-up world that doesn't know if it's coming or going, is no "bed of roses." I can tell you this much: Life, including the Christian experience, is anything but soft and serene. Jesus both warned and comforted His followers:

> **John 16:33, AMP** – *"I have told you these things, so that in Me you may have [perfect] peace. In the world you have tribulation and distress and suffering, but be courageous [be confident, be undaunted, be filled with joy]; I have overcome the world [My conquest is accomplished, My victory abiding]."*

Jesus informed His disciples that the Christian life was intended to be different and exceptional, or at least it should be. It was and is meant to be lived, not in defeat, but in triumph. The follower of Christ is to stand up, toughen up, and courageously buck up against the sufferings and foolishness of this present age. After all, we are connected to, in union with, an omnipotent, sovereign God, Who is at war on our behalf, conquering everything the world, the flesh, or the devil might throw our way. Jesus used the word *"overcome"* (to conquer, prevail, victorious in battle).[12] It was meant to be a word of encouragement, designed to instill a deep sense of inner peace and a quiet joy, come what may. It was a

---

[12] William F. Arndt and F> Wilbur Gingrich, *A Greek-English Lexicon of the New Testament and Other Early Christian Literature,* (Chicago, Illinois: The University of Chicago Press, 1957), 541.

promise of victory to men and women whose world was about to collapse.

But Jesus doesn't stop there. He is a realist. Always has been. There is nothing more real than the cross, the centerpiece of Christianity. *"The emblem of suffering and shame,"* a picture of our daily experiences, trials, temptations, suffering, sacrifice, imprisonment, and beatings. Nothing too "grand" about any of that. A friend of mine once said, "One of the many things that I appreciate about Christianity is that its founder was very plain spoken and truthful when he told his disciples that *'in this world you are going to have trouble.'* I'm also reminded of the fact that over three fourths of the Psalms contain complaints to God."[13]

Mother Theresa, who "worked herself to the bone," spent her life in service to the poor, the sick, the lame, society's most destitute and needy. She wrote in a letter to God, "In the call [God's call to a lifetime of ministry], You said that I would have to suffer much."[14] And suffer she did, seeing and touching the lives of broken people on the streets and slums of Calcutta. There were many, and she had no means or resources to adequately meet their needs. Distraught, discouraged, desperate, and overwhelmed by the immense burden of ministry and her own inadequacies, she said, "In my soul, I feel that terrible pain of loss – of God not wanting me- of God not being God- of God not really existing."[15] She suffered deeply for the people she was called to serve.

Paul reminded the church at Rome that *"All of creation is groaning until the day of redemption"* (Romans 8:22). For some, life is just plain frightening, filled with uncertainty, anxiety, and fears. It reeks of tragedy! And Paul knew it. Life can hurt badly! The

---

[13] Used by permission.
[14] Jim Towey, *To Love and Be Loved*, (New York, NY: Simon & Schuster Paperbacks, 2022), 171.
[15] Ibid.

poet, Robert Burns, informs us that in this life the best laid plans of mice and men often go awry with disastrous results.[16]

Jessica, a mother of two, went to the doctor for her four-month check-up. She was pregnant with her third child and "excited to be having another baby and...a new member in the family." This time she was hoping for a girl. The doctor did the exam but could not find a heartbeat. The monitor showed a flat line. The baby had died in the womb. The news was heartbreaking, and Jessica, distraught and grieving, thought to end her own life. She wrote on Quora (a platform for asking and answering questions):

> *I was angry. Angry that God took my baby. I was so hurt and angry that God would take something so precious from me that I almost killed myself. I was going to run my car straight into a tree at full speed. I acted out in ways I shouldn't have all to hurt God the way he hurt me. In the end, I saw that I was only hurting myself.*
>
> *Unfortunate things happen in this world. Things we can't wrap our heads around...I was able to muster up a prayer (a prayer everybody asks God in one form or another)... "Dear Heavenly Father, 'Why?' Help me understand. I'm angry and hurt. Please help." Believing in God doesn't mean that we will be shielded from all of life's hurts.*[17]

How right she is.

Here is a short list of questions I have compiled for this book, presented in no particular order. There is nothing new here. They are certainly commonplace among fellow journey men and women,

---

[16] Robert Burns, To a Mouse (November 1785), *Poetry Foundation*, retrieved from https://www.poetryfoundation.org/poems/43816/to-a-mouse-56d222ab36e33.

[17] Retrieved from Quora https://www.quora.com/What-is-the-point-of-believing-in-God-besides-hopefully-not-going-to-hell-My-mom-died-too-early-and-Im-mad-at-God-I-dont-want-to-be-but-I-am-I-did-finally-go-to-church-but-its-still-hard-to-pray-I-am-feeling-lost. No date. No copyright.

who have been weeping for years over the events they've experienced in their lives. They are the questions I've asked of God myself at one point or another in my own story. I'm sure you can relate to some, if not all, and add to the list below.

1. God, where were You when I needed You?
2. Don't You care? Don't You love me?
3. Why so much pain and suffering in the world?
4. How is this helping me? What purpose does it serve?
5. How could You let this happen?
6. When will You call the dogs off?
7. What have I done to deserve this? What did I do?[18]

This book was written with a good deal of fear and trepidation, keeping in mind the brokenhearted and the spiritually wounded and those who have a "real problem" with God – all screaming for answers of which I have so little. My hope, however, is that the stories and words recorded within these pages will be used by the great Healer and Comforter to restore your spiritual footing, find some solace for your soul, renew your faith and trust in God, and deepen your relationship with the only One Who truly loves and cares for you.

To all such people, Elizabeth Elliot wrote:

One often hears people say, "The first question I'm going to ask God when I get to heaven is . . ." (and you can fill in the blank). During His final discourse with the disciples before He went to the cross, they were asking Him many questions. Jesus said to them, "Now is your time of grief, but I will see you again and you will rejoice, and no one will take away your joy...There are not many new questions in our very human hearts .(God has heard them all). When I

---

[18] Tod Perry, People are sharing the 'one question' they'd ask God if they could and the responses are deep, *Up Worthy*, April 22, 2022, https://www.upworthy.com/most-important-van-in-nyc-full-of-bombas-socks

> *examine my own heart and find that I am tempted to say to the Lord, "Yes, but—" or "What about—?" or "How can I possibly—?" I find that He has questions for me: Are you willing to understand? To rearrange your life? To be healed? To lose your life for my sake? Do you want solutions or holiness? Answers or orders? The light of Christ or your own logic? I must ask myself: Do I treat the truth of God as though it were something to be tinkered with or something to be submitted to?... Evelyn Underhill puts it this way: 'It is only disguised pride that makes us fret over what we can't understand.' God will see to it that we understand as much truth as we are willing to obey.[19]*

The chapters that follow will attempt to deal honestly and openly with some of the questions we throw at God. The list is not meant to be exhaustive, but they are common questions asked among men and women from every walk of life, the high and the mighty, the rich and the poor, the privileged, the lowly, the prince and the servant, the sick and the healthy, and the young and the old. Pain comes to everyone. There is no escape. Nobody is immune. Tragedy and heartache are no respecter of people. There is an abundance of *"weeping and gnashing of teeth"* (Matthew 8:12, NASB) to be found in this fallen world, enough to go around for everybody. Life is no joke. I wish it were not so.

In one of the climactic scenes from J.R.R. Tolkien's trilogy, *The Lord of the Rings,* the young hobbit, Frodo, weeps over the world he sees around him with all the tragedy and darkness he and his companions have had to endure. "I wish the ring had never come to me," he mournfully admitted. The past was dismal, the present troublesome, and the future did not appear to be much better. Frodo lamented, "I wish it need not have happened in my time."

---

[19] Elizabeth Elliot, *Secure in the Everlasting Arms,* Kindle Edition, (Grand Rapids, Michigan: Revell, 2002), 22.

Gandalf the Wise consoled his young protégé, "So do I, and all who live to see such times, but that is not for them to decide. All we have to decide is what to do with the time that is given to us. There are other forces at work in this world, Frodo, besides the will of evil."

Comforting words.

There are things I wish had not happened in my life, too. Regrets are routine and painful in and of themselves. What I decide to do with those hard and difficult experiences is the difference between living each day victoriously or dying a slow painful, agonizing death within my being. I must make a decision, which way shall I go, who can I trust as I journey through this world, especially when adversity and suffering invade my daily routines and strikes a hard blow that hurts deeply. Maybe we wounded souls can learn to trust God once again in the most mundane and terrible circumstances of life and avoid the error of interrogating the King.

Let the questions be brought to the throne room of God. He can handle them there. Go ahead, demand your audience. You will discover soon enough the biblical truth behind the Afro-American spiritual, *He's Got the Whole World in His Hands,* and that includes you and me. It's the answer we've been looking for all along.

> *In the darkness you could hear the shrieks of women, the screams of children, and the shouts of men; some calling for their children, others for their parents, others for their husbands one lamenting his own fate, another that of his family; some wishing to die, from the very fear of dying; some lifting their hands to the gods; but the greater part convinced that there were now no gods at all, and that the final endless night of which we have heard had come upon the world.*[20]
>
> – Pliny the Younger, A.D. 79, the eruption of Mt. Vesuvius near Pompeii

CHAPTER 1

God, Where Were You When I Needed You?

Some time ago, a former student-athlete of mine wrote me a letter. He had lost both his parents – one to cancer and the other a year later to a tragic car accident. I was at both funerals and left weeping for that boy. He was just a teenager, eighteen years old at the time. He sent me the following letter a year or so later:

> *I've been doing some thinking lately about my relationship to Christ. Sometimes I'm feeling it, and everything is like sunshine and roses. Then, there are days when I feel like I'm at the bottom of the canyon, like now. I feel like I'm in the woods turning around and looking for Jesus, but not seeing Him.*
>
> *Right now, I feel like God has forgotten me. I'm thinking that God just can't hear me because He*

---
[20] The two letters written by Pliny the younger to his uncle (Tacticus) about the eruption of Vesuvius in 79 A.D., *History of Pompeii*, retrieved from http://www.pompeii.org.uk/s.php/tour-the-two-letters-written-by-pliny-the-elder-about-the-eruption-of-vesuvius-in-79-a-d-history-of-pompeii-en-238-s.htm.

doesn't know me. I just don't know what to do. All I know is that this is not how God intended me to live.

An honest account. These are the thoughts of a broken, scared, young man, grappling with his loss and feeling like God had let him down. The cruelty and darkness of death decimated a family. It always does. He felt isolated and afraid, wondering what to do, where to go, and what would become of him. The home and family he once knew were gone. Everything had changed and not for the better. The God he thought he could depend on to hold things together and see him through seemed to have abandoned him. God had vanished from the scene. At least, that's how he felt—alone and on his own. He needed help. He needed God, and as far as he was concerned, God was nowhere to be found.

David wrote the thirteenth Psalm which records the words of a man in anguish, a man feeling forsaken, forlorn, and forgotten in this world, a man looking for answers but not finding any. Four times David asked, *"How long?"* We are unsure of the historical event or occasion behind the psalm, but we do know that whatever David was going through it left him terribly depressed, wanting and waiting for God to step in and remedy the situation. And so he wrote:

> **Psalm 13:1-3, NLT** *– O Lord, how long will you forget me? Forever? How long will you look the other way? How long must I struggle with anguish in my soul, with sorrow in my heart every day? How long will my enemy have the upper hand? Turn and answer me, O Lord my God! Restore the sparkle to my eyes, or I will die.*

That's how he felt. That's how I have felt. C.H. Spurgeon commented on this Psalm, challenging our foolish thinking and attitudes. He goes right to the heart of the matter when he wrote:

> *Ah, David! How like a fool thou talkest! Can God forget? Can omniscience fail in (God's) memory?*

> *Above all, can Jehovah's heart forget His own beloved child? Ah, brethren, let us drive away the thought...*[21]

It is an awful place to be, feeling alone and thinking you are on your own, hopeless, and cut off from the love and presence of God. Like so many, David's dream of a better tomorrow had vanished. He lay in the dust of his own anguish, demoralized, defeated, and ready to throw in the towel, quit on life, quit on himself, and quit on God. In short, the man was dead on the inside, the *sparkle* gone. But read the rest of the Psalm. David doesn't stay down for long.

The sons of Korah sang a similar tune (Psalm 88), a song we are all too familiar with in this life: *"I've had my fill of trouble, I'm camped on the edge of hell...I'm caught in a maze and can't find my way out"* (Psalm 88:1-9, MSG). I have sung a similar song through gritted teeth and tears in my eyes, feeling much like that young man who said that he was *"turning around and looking for Jesus, but not seeing Him."* Indeed, where is God when I need Him? It is a common complaint among common men and women living in a world gone crazy.

A 2018 survey by the Pew Research Center indicated that 56% of Americans said, "I talk to God and God does not talk back."[22] To some, God is either absent from the scene, He doesn't care, He's incapable of connecting meaningfully with any of us, or He is void of sufficient power to make a real difference in our lives. None of which is true, though at times, it may seem otherwise.

Regardless of my situation, no matter how messy life has gotten, or how bad I hurt, God speaks to my pain, *"I will not forget you."* His Word is comforting. *"Behold, I have inscribed you on the palms of My hands"* (Isaiah 49:14-16, NASB). That's a good place to be, never far from God's mind, always in His thoughts and in His

---

[21] David Otis Fuller, *C.H. Spurgeon's Treasure of David*, (Grand Rapids, Michigan, 1940), 57.
[22] Editor, We Believe in God, CT magazine (June, 2018), p. 15

plans, and living daily under His protection and in the context of His purpose for my life. There I can take refuge amid life's hardships and challenges and do so confidently in the shadow of His wings (Psalm 91:1-4). John A. Broadus, founder and the 2nd president of the Southern Baptist Theological Seminary (1889-1895), said:

> *We cannot fully understand now, but when we stand upon the heights of glory, we shall look back with joy on the things we suffered, for we shall know then that our severest trials were a part of the "all things" which work together for eternal good.*[23]

In this life, it is a hard sell, but it is the truth, nonetheless.

Some years ago, I attended a military memorial service at Fort Campbell, KY, for a young man. Kyle was his name. I officiated at his memorial service in Ft. Worth, TX, for family and friends. Five to six to hundred people were in attendance to honor the life of this young man, and I had the distinct privilege of preaching his funeral. What an honor.

Kyle had been awarded the Bronze Star for heroic service in a combat zone and the Medal of Valor twice for his courage under fire on the battlefield. He was one of my former soccer players at Bryan College. A quality young man. One of America's finest. After a long courageous, two-year battle with esophageal cancer, he died at thirty years of age, leaving behind a loving wife and a two-year-old daughter. It was tragic and gut wrenching, to say the least. Frustrated and furious at God, his mother cried to me:

> *I prayed, fasted, read my Bible; believed that God would heal him. I begged God for my son's life…and look at where we are! I'm so angry at God. I'm not opening my Bible. I don't want to talk to Him, not now…not after this!*

---

[23] John Albert Broadus, Author Quotes, *Goodreads*, No date, retrieved from https://www.goodreads.com/author/quotes/662692.John_Albert_Broadus.

Can you blame her? Such deep pain. A mother's heart laid bare. All I could say quietly was, "It's okay. Go ahead. God is bigger than your anger." I had nothing else. I could do little more than just listen, which was probably best. It was not the occasion for Christian platitudes. They never work very well anyway. There are times when answers are hard to come by, and this was one of those harrowing moments.

When the quality of our faith is put to the test, we need God more than ever, plain and simple. In the quietness of our soul, where turmoil and anxiousness invade, we need Him to pour into our emptiness and wounds the healing *"balm of Gilead"* (Jeremiah 8:22). We need His reassurance, His strength, His compassion, His hope, His Word, and His grace for the day. God will meet us at the point of desperation and despair.

Shortly after his wife died, Charles Allen, the noted United Methodist pastor and author, wrote a book entitled, *Victory in the Valleys of Life* (Revell, 1981). He told the story of five-year-old Johnny. Johnny was in the kitchen one afternoon, watching his mother make supper when she asked him to go into the pantry down the hall and get her a can of tomato soup. It was the last place he wanted to go alone.

He said, "It's dark in there. I'm scared, and I'm not going."

His mother pressed him a bit more, but he dug his heels in. He refused to go farther. Finally, a bit frustrated, she said, "It's okay, Jesus will be in there with you."

Well, Johnny started back down the hallway slowly, reluctantly, and cautiously.

He stopped at the door. Reached for the knob, turned it, and gently opened it. He peeked inside. It was still dark. He thought for a moment. Then shook his head as if to say, "No way," and started to close the door behind him. But he stopped. Turned around. Then shouted, "Jesus, if you're in there, hand me out that can of tomato soup!"[24]

That's precisely what we must have when terrified of the dark that envelops us. Not the can of soup, but the assurance of the presence of God in our lives to get us through the darkest of hours. He is not some distant god, who is disinterested, uninvolved, or uncaring about what's going on in my daily life or yours. He is no abstract, no theological concept, no illusion. He is for real!

He showed up for the good times at a wedding feast, and turned water into the finest of wines simply because He could and because His mother needed Him. He traveled to the tomb of Lazarus and poured the breath of life back into the mouth of a corpse with but His word, and transformed a funeral, where grief and sorrow ruled, to a place of celebration and renewed faith in God.

Not once has God ever left me to my own devices to deal with life's hardships. Never. In fact, He gets down, deep and dirty into the trenches where I live – in my disappointments, my despair, my heartache, my diseases, my failures, my troubles, my pain, and my fears. *"Even though I walk through the valley of the shadow (deep darkness) of death (evil)…Thou art with me"* (Psalm 23:4). Good news for the troubled soul.

God has been seen jumping into a fiery furnace with a few of His buddies. He has done that a lot over the years. He was in the lion's den at lunchtime with His friend, Daniel. He was in a storm off the shore of Malta on a ship that went down with His servant Paul. God is along for the ride everywhere you look. He came strolling on the sea in the midst of raging winds and pounding waves to stand shoulder-to-shoulder with His disciples and quieted their fears. He was out on the battlefield with a ruddy-faced kid named, David, who had but a sling and a few stones to oppose a giant

---

[24] Brett Petrillo (BP), Are we afraid of the dark?" *BP's Fuel for Thought* (Blog), November 10, 2015, retrieved from
https://bpsfuelforthought.wordpress.com/2015/11/10/are-we-afraid-of-the-dark/.

nobody thought could ever be beaten. When a few believers were locked away in a room in the back alleyways of Jerusalem for *"fear of the Jews* (the religious rulers of the day), John records that Jesus *"came and stood in their midst"* (John 20:19). He simply showed up, again and again.

Death and the grave could not cut Him off from those He loved. He was there *"in the midst,"* (literally, *"in the middle"*) of their worries and fears. He was there on the shores of the Red Sea when Pharoah's war chariots closed in for the kill. God was there at the battle for Jericho and shook the walls of the city to the ground. He was there with Joseph, jailed for something he didn't do. He was there in the mud pits of Egypt for four hundred years making bricks with Jewish slaves. God was floating down the Nile in a basket with a baby boy named Moses (more on him in another chapter), who later would become Israel's greatest leader, and successfully marched the people through the wilderness and onto the banks of the Jordan. God was there at every step. A cloud guided them during the day. A pillar of fire protected them in the night.

He was with John Wycliffe (1377-1384) who believed that every Christian should have a Bible in their hands, and then translated the Scriptures into English against heavy opposition. God climbed the scaffold with Donald Cargill (1681), a Presbyterian pastor who was beheaded in Scotland for the sake of the Gospel. As he mounted the ladder on the scaffold, he was heard to say, "Lord knows I go up this ladder with less fear and anxiety than I ever entered the pulpit to preach." No man faces his end with such courage apart from the presence and empowering of God, who stood with him on that scaffold when the fires were lit. God stood with Martin Luther when he nailed his 95 theses (1517) to the Castle Church door at Whittenburg, denouncing the abuses of indulgences. God has been with every Old and New Testament believer through thick and thin from the inception of mankind and beyond, and He is here now in your life and mine. At no time was/is God ever "missing in action."

Several years ago, I had a heart attack. The day after surgery, I awoke early in the ICU (before the nurses started their rounds). As I opened my eyes to meet the day, an old church hymn filled my mind and reassured my soul. Laying in a hospital bed, I was flat on my back, looking in the only direction I could, upward, trying to peer through the concrete ceiling and reach the heavens. I was alone, so I thought, and began to sing to myself in a whisper:

> *Blessed assurance, Jesus is mine.*
> *Oh what a foretaste of glory divine.*
> *Heir of salvation; purchased of God:*
> *Born of His Spirit; washed in His blood.*
> *This is my story* [It could be yours, too];
> *this is MY song* [You can sing along, if you wish]
> *Praising my Savior all the day long...*

The words of that great hymn washed over me like waves of cool ocean water on a hot summer day at the Jersey Shore. My spirit was refreshed. The presence of God was strong in that hospital room. I was at peace. No fears. No anxiety. No doubts. Just rejoicing quietly because *"the Lord was near"* (Philippians 4:4-5), and I knew it. He is present in the good times and the bad.

Mary and Martha understood the significance and necessity of the presence and power of God in their lives. Their brother, Lazarus, fell deathly sick. So, the sisters called for Jesus (I would have done the same), the only One they knew Who could step in and save his life. Twice, the Gospel of John mentions that Jesus *loved* this family (John 11:3, 5). *"Yet, when He heard that Lazarus was sick, He stayed where he was two more days"* (John 11:6). The implications of the decision to stay put are disconcerting. I am very uncomfortable reading those words. God could have helped. Instead, the God of this universe, the King of kings Who rules overall and holds the power of life and death in His hands, delays

His response. The omnipotent, miracle-working God, the great I AM, Who brought mighty Egypt to its knees, the Good Shepherd Who loves and cares for His sheep chooses not to act, not to intervene, and does so deliberately, purposely, and intentionally. He just sits and waits and lets things run their course. I absolutely must do the same...wait on God, which might be the toughest of all spiritual exercises, for I have my own timetable.

As expected, the inevitable takes place. Lazarus dies (John 11:14), and we think that God was too late, that somehow, He missed His opportunity to show case His kindness and compassion and meet the needs of the people He loved. But God loves surprises. He always has. His delays become our daily adventure with Christ and an occasion to grow spiritually, mature more in the faith, and glorify His name before a watching world. The once captain of a slave ship, John Newton, who wrote *Amazing Grace,* said it this way:

> *Trials are medicines which our great and wise Physician prescribes because we need them. He proportions the frequency and weight of them to what our case requires. Let us trust in His skill, and thank him for His prescriptions.*[25]

By the time Jesus arrived on the scene, Lazarus had been dead four days and his body had already begun to rot in the tomb. In the mind of every Jew weeping at the gravesite that day, there was no doubt: the man was deader than a rock.

If there is one thing I've learned in the last seventy seven years it is this: God is profoundly unpredictable. He does the unexpected. He will not be controlled nor coerced or coaxed into doing what He does not want to do, no matter how loud I shout, how high I jump,

---

[25] John Newton, "Let us trust our physician," *Tolle Lege (Take up and Read)*, August 21, 2015, retrieved from https://tollelege.net/2015/08/21/let-us-trust-our-physician-by-john-newton/#:~:text=Trials%20therefore%20are%20medicines%2C%20which,to%20what%20the%20case%20requires .

or how many tears I shed. He acts in ways that often confound me, even offend me. He is not sympathetic with my lack of understanding or my bruised feelings. He does as He pleases, when He pleases, and where He pleases for reasons well beyond my pay grade. Along the way, I've also discovered that God doesn't need my help with anything, nor does He seek my approval, though I stand ready to serve as His personal advisor. I confess my arrogance. I have readily and repeatedly applied for the position of "Fourth Member of the Trinity" so I might help the All-knowing, All-wise, All-powerful God out of a jam and straighten-out His thinking. By the way, that application is still pending, though I'm expecting the job offer on my desk most any day now...yes, it's an absurd, ridiculous notion, but I've done it, and so have you.

Seriously, God does according to His good pleasure and plans, not mine, which, by the way, serves only to muddy my theology. Frankly, He has every right as the King to call the shots and so order my steps, whether I agree or disagree, understand or misunderstand the path He has chosen for my life and that of the people I love. His heavenly schemes, His pure motives, His perfect will and holy purpose remain a perplexing blueprint of design for finite minds trying to grasp divine actions born in the mystery of the Godhead. Infinity, eternity, immensity, and all the rest, are beyond my comprehension. I don't get it. Who does outside of God Himself?

Neither did Mary and Martha, who begged for their brother's life. They knew Jesus had the ability to save Lazarus. *"For with God nothing is ever impossible and no word from God shall be without power"* (Luke 1:37, AMPC). Jesus was their Man. There was no doubt in their minds. They had witnessed and certainly heard of the unleashing of God's omnipotent power in the villages and streets of the ancient world. They knew the stories. The blind now see. The lame now walk. The dead rise. The hungry are fed. Broken bodies have been made whole. All manner of diseases has been healed. Even the demons of hell cower before His authority and fall at His feet in fear when He arrived on the scene. Obviously, God could turn things around, if He had a mind to do it, and perform the miracle those women so desperately needed and wanted. But He doesn't. He doesn't lift a finger. How very unnerving. Seems more common than uncommon.

In his devotional, *God Is With You Every Day,* Max Lucado, challenges us to think rightly, biblically, and more deeply about who God is and what He is able to do and wants to do in our daily lives. He writes:

> *Most people suffer from small thoughts about God. In an effort to see him as our friend, we have lost his immensity. In our desire to understand him, we have sought to contain him. The God of the Bible cannot be contained. He brought order out of chaos and created creation. With a word he created Adam out of dust and Eve out of bone. He consulted no committee. He sought no counsel.*
>
> *He has no peer. 'I am God, and there is none like me' (Isaiah 46:9, NIV)...From the tiniest microbe to the mightiest mountain 'he sustains everything by the mighty power of his command' (Hebrews 1:3, NLT).*
>
> *He has authority over the world and...He has authority over your world. He's never surprised. And He has never, ever uttered the phrase, 'How did that happen?'* [26]

The two sisters who never thought small about Jesus, twice said to Him, *"If only you had been here!"* (John 11: 21, 32). In some ways, they acknowledged His power and authority over all things. Yet, their words seemingly betrayed their disillusionment and disappointment. Lazarus' death may have been perceived as God's failure to meet their needs in the most terrifying moments of their lives. *"God, where were You when we needed You?"*

---

[26] Lucado, Max. *God Is With You Every Day*, Thomas Nelson. Kindle Edition, 227-228

C.S. Lewis, one of Christianity's greatest thinkers and philosophers of the twentieth century, authored a book entitled, *A Grief Observed*. In the forward of that book, there is the record of Lewis' honest, but brutal response to the death of his beloved wife. He asked what so many of us have wanted to know – an all too familiar question:

> *Where is God?... go to Him when your need is desperate, when all other help is vain, and what do you find? A door slammed in your face, and a sound of bolting and double-bolting on the inside.*
>
> *After that, silence...the conclusion I dread is not 'so there's no God after all,' but 'so this is what God's really like. Deceive yourself no longer.*[27]

We know that Lewis eventually moved past the loss of his wife, but the depth of such acute pain remains unmistakable and universal. Grief and sorrow seems unbearable, and the "shadow of death" overwhelms daily life. Apart from Christ, death *"stings"* (1 Corinthians 15:55). It breaks the heart and kills the spirit.

Elie Wiesel, a Jewish prisoner in the Auschwitz and Buchenwald concentration camps of World War II, wrote what many consider to be a masterpiece. He entitled it simply, *Night* (Hill and Wang, 2006). It is a candid and terrifying account of his survival as a teenager in the Nazi camps. In his book, Wiesel described an unforgettable scene in graphic terms. Conditions were so horrific and merciless, he once said, "Never shall I forget the flames [the ovens] that consumed my faith forever...Never shall I forget those moments that murdered my God."

The entire camp was assembled in the yard to witness the hanging of three Jewish prisoners. The trumped-up charges were read by the executioner. Each of the three victims were then required to mount a chair placed in front of them. A noose was slipped over

---

[27] C.S. Lewis, *A Grief Observed*, (Greenwich, Connecticut: The Leabury Press, 1963), 9.

their respective heads, and the chairs were tipped over upon command. There was total silence throughout the camp as several thousand prisoners, frozen in fear and terror, were forced to watch the gruesome spectacle take place. One of the accused was a young Dutch boy who thrashed about for thirty minutes before death mercifully came.

Someone standing behind Elie whispered, "For God's sake, where is God? Where is He? Where is God now?"

Wiesel later wrote, "I heard a voice within me answer him: 'Where is He [God]? Here He is? He is hanging here on these gallows."[28]

The psalmist asked:

> **Psalms 139:7-12, TPT** – *Where could I go from your Spirit?* [nowhere] *Where could I run and hide from Your face?* [Again, nowhere]. *If I go up to heaven, you're there. If I go down to the realm of the dead* [even a Nazi death camp], *You're there too! If I fly with wings into the shining dawn, you're there* [every morning when I rise to face the day]. *If I fly into the radiant sunset* [when night approaches], *you're there waiting! Wherever I go, your hand will guide me; Your strength will empower me* [to move forward]. *It's impossible to disappear from you or to ask the darkness to hide me, for your presence is everywhere, bringing light into my night. There is no such thing as darkness with you. The night, to you, is as bright as the day* [He is never surprised]; *there's no difference between the two.*

There is no hiding from God. There is no place where I can go where God is not. He is much closer than you or I think! He goes before me. He stands behind me. He is to my right hand and to my left. He is above me and below me. He is a *"shield around me, My glory, and the One who lifts my head"* (Psalm 3:3, NASB). He

---
[28] Elie Wiesel, *Night* (New York, New York: Hill and Wang, 2012), 8-9 (Kindle).

surrounds me with His *"favor"* (Psalm 5:12), and His Spirit is resident within me. He is here and there before eternity began. He will be here and there *"from everlasting to everlasting"* (Psalm 93:2). However you say it, that's a long, long time. I just can't seem to shake God.

In 1902, Charles A. Tindley became the pastor of Bainbridge Street Methodist Church in Philadelphia. It was "the church where he was converted…and once served as a janitor" to support his wife and three children. He was not a learned man, but he taught himself to read and write—a remarkable feat given the fact that schooling for a Black boy was prohibited. Later, he "enrolled in theology classes, learned Greek, and studied Hebrew with a local Rabbi,"[29] all the while serving as pastor of a local church. He was a busy man.

Life was never easy for Charles. He was no stranger to heartbreak and pain. Two of his children passed away in 1882 and 1909. Hester, his one-year-old daughter died of croup pneumonia, and Irene died at the age of thirteen from tuberculosis. Yet, Tindley maintained his faith and commitment to God despite the sorrow of his losses. His faith never wavered throughout those tough, hard days. He stayed the course and set himself to build the Kingdom of God where God had placed him. Incredible courage and uncommon fortitude. Tindley spent many a day standing on the street corners of Philly, talking to anyone who would listen to the good news of God's "saving grace." He was tenacious and driven to proclaim Christ and touch the hearts of people in need of God's love, forgiveness, and mercy. His ability to communicate drew national attention, as did his commitment and work to remedy social ills.

He started a ministry for the homeless when it wasn't fashionable to do so, opened soup kitchens to feed the poor, and started a financial service to benefit those in poverty. His thirty-year

---

[29]Christina J. Thomas, The Biography of Charles Albert Tindley, *Diary Of A Historian*, May 5, 2015, retrieved from https://diaryofahistorian.com/2015/05/05/we-shall-overcome-the-biography-of-charles-albert-tindley/

ministry began with two hundred church members and eventually grew to over ten thousand in attendance.[30] A new church building was purchased to accommodate the crowds. The night before the scheduled dedication of the facility, Charles' wife, Daisy, died suddenly, a tragic, heartbreaking loss for a man who had served God throughout his adult life. Amid the despair and sadness over his wife's death and under the enormous strain and pressure of leadership and heavy opposition to his ministry, Tindley sat down and penned the following words written as a prayer and set to music. *Stand By Me* was one of forty-six Gospel songs he wrote.

> *When the storms of life are raging, stand by me...*
> *When the world is tossing me like a ship upon the sea*
> *Thou Who rulest wind and water, stand by me.*
>
> *In the midst of tribulation, stand by me...*
> *When the hosts of hell assail,*
> *And my strength begins to fail*
> *Thou Who never lost a battle, stand by me.*[31]

God has always stood by me. He has never kept His distance from me. He has never stood back, nor backed away from me, but moves closer and presses in on my life.

Where is God when I need Him most? In the darkness of the night, in the deepest regions of my soul. There I can find Him *"bringing light into my night"* (Psalm 139). There I can see Him, feel Him, and trust Him, for He "stands by me" always and forever. *"God hasn't left (my) side"* (2 Corinthians 4:9, MSG), and neither has He left yours.

---

[30] Ibid.
[31] Robert J Morgan, *150 of the World's Greatest Hymn Stories: Then Sings My Soul, Book II*, (Nashville, Tennessee: Thomas Nelson, Inc, 2004), 251.

WHERE IS GOD?

Yet when he (Jesus) heard that Lazarus was sick, he stayed where he was two more days... Lazarus is dead. –John 11:6, 14, NIV

*Where is God
When I need Him;
When life gets|
Dangerous,|
Downright dreadful,
Diseased,
Deadly,
Depressing?
When
Moments of unexpected,
Unimaginable
Heartbreak
and horror
Intrude
Invade,
Impede my daily routine.
Assaulting my faith
Pressing hard against
the boundaries of sanity and sanctity.
My mind wanders down dark,
Crooked paths.
Wondering if God will step in,
Waiting for things to get better,
Wishing things were different.
How often have I
Whined, "Unfair!"
Screamed, "Unjust!"
Cried, "Pointless!"
When the thing feared most comes upon me.
"Where is God?"
The heart weeps,
"Lord, if only You were here..."
The desperate,*

mournful words of two hurting souls,
Mary and Martha,
Who thought...
God could have done something,
should have done something.
Mercifully,
Jesus shows up at tombs.
*He **likes** doing that.*
Count on it.
In hospital rooms,
The marketplace,
The unemployment lines.
The divorce courts.
No!
I am not alone... ever!
I am not forgotten...
My name has been written on the palms of Almighty
God (Isaiah 49:16).
The Resurrection and the Life (John 11:25)
Rises,
Redeems,
Rescues.
Rules.
The God who has never run from pain,
especially mine,
is near.
In the pits of despair
In loneliness and isolation,
In the courts of false accusations and rejection.
In a battle with fierce giants,
Courage comes to win the day.
FINALLY,
like the countless saints of old,
I can begin to
recline,
relax some,
rejoice,
"For the Lord is near." (Philippians 4:5)

The truth declared.
"He is risen!" *(Matthew 28:6)*
And once again,
the heavens trumpet God's promise
across the universe.
"I am with you always,
even to the end of the age" (Matthew 28:20),
To
STAND BY YOU,
STAND WITH YOU
STAND UP FOR YOU.
Where is God?
The answer is certain.
In troubled waters.
Where is God?
In the furnace.
Where is God?
In the arena where a man's faith is severely tested.
Where is God?
*He is **NEAR!***
*He is **THERE!***
*He is **HERE!***
Now and forevermore.
*Let the **PEACE** of God reign supreme.*
–Sandy

> *Everyone has noticed how hard it is to turn our thoughts to God when everything is going well with us. We 'have all we want' is a terrible saying when 'all' does not include God. We find God an interruption... We regard God as an airman regards his parachute; it's for emergencies but he hopes he'll never have to use it."*
>
> –C.S. Lewis, The Problem of Pain, 1940

CHAPTER 2

Don't You Care? Why Don't You love me?

In his book, *Disappointment with God*, Philip Yancey quoted a friend whose life was out of control, a bewildered, anxious, skeptical man. His future was uncertain, and daily life seemed downright dismal. He asked Yancey, "Does God really care? If so, why won't He reach down and fix the things that go wrong at least some of them?"[32] The question is so very human, so familiar to us all.

I walk nearly every day in the local mall, which has allowed me the opportunity and privilege to befriend a number of merchants. I recently asked one of them, "If you could ask God one question, what would it be? What would you say to God if you were standing in front of Him right now?"

He blurted out, "What's my purpose in life? Why am I here? I haven't a clue."

---

[32] Philip Yancey, Disappointment with God: Two Best Sellers in one Volume, (Zondervan, 1988), 35.

A few hours later, he texted me another question for God to answer. He asked, "God, why don't You love me? Actually, I'm pretty pissed-off right now." Colorful language, but nevertheless a passionate, genuine, and troublesome response. He meant it…every word. He was a man in his fifties, in a going-nowhere job, and slowly dying on the inside. To exasperate his anger, he has been at times suicidal, was a product of incest, was floundering, bewildered, without a meaningful direction in life, and feeling uncared for and unloved by family and the few he once thought to be friends. Worst of all, he felt betrayed by the one Person (God) he believed could surely have done something about his situation but Who chose not to intervene and act.

As we talked, it struck me that he was taking no personal responsibility for the life he was now living (and I told him so) or for the decisions he made as a younger man (the parties he attended, the drugs he used, and the heavy drinking he continued to brag about), all of which contributed heavily to his current state. He was bitter and angry at a God he wasn't sure even existed (which I found rather ironic) and blamed Him for his hapless state. Clearly, he believed God was at fault. God had let him down. God did not love him, otherwise he wouldn't be in his predicament of being divinely duped, forgotten by God, and a product of God's disregard for his well-being. Consequently, he thought of himself as helpless, an innocent victim, useless and worthless, discouraged in life, and disappointed with himself and God, thus not good enough to ever warrant God's attention or favor.

I could readily understand how he thought as he did. My heart broke for him, especially as he rolled up his sleeves to show me the scars on his wrists from the day he tried to end his misery. He was a lonely, hurting man who has been discarded by society and left to die a thousand deaths before his feet ever hit the grave.

However, the fact is that God *does* love the unlovely. No strings attached. His arms are open wide to all, the good, the bad, and the ugly. He loves the successful and the failure, the highly talented and the ordinary guy. God loves them all, the business tycoon and the street peddler playing his violin in the subway for a few extra coins, the person betrayed by his/her best friend and the one affirmed and accepted, the strong and the weak, those who weep and those who rejoice…everybody, from every walk of life, culture, background, and generation. No exceptions. *"God is not one to show partiality"* (Acts 10:34, NASB). The love of God for all humanity (including my friend at the mall) is and will forever be boundless. His love is "deep and wide" (an old Sunday school chorus), timeless, eternal, without measure, unrelenting, and compelling. It has the power to change a hopelessly wretched life, put a bounce back in one's step, clear up muddied thinking, give hope to the less fortunate, inject dignity and self-esteem into an empty soul, and restore *"my passion for life"* (Psalm 51:12, TPT). Psalm 51 was written by King David in the throes of his guilt and shame over his adulterous affair with Bathsheba and his murder of her husband. There is hope for me and you.

There is but one place where you and I can catch a glimpse of the magnitude, splendor, and depth of the grace, mercy, and lovingkindness of God. On a hill called Golgotha, the Cross stands in love eternal, overshadowing all the universe and, in particular, your life and mine. There is no question. "Calvary is the one objective, absolute, irrefutable proof of God's love for us."[33] There, on an altar of blood stained wood, God freely gave His son as a substitutionary atonement to pay for the sins of a bunch of screw-ups and yahoos (and that especially includes yours truly), rebels every one of us, a self-centered, selfish lot in great need of forgiveness and mercy for the mess we've made of our lives and the world we live in.

---

[33] Jerry Bridges, *Christian Quotes*, retrieved from https://www.christianquotes.info/top-quotes/19-important-quotes-about-the-cross/. Jerry Bridges was an author, speaker and staff member of The Navigators.

John Grisham's 1999 novel, *The Testament*, is fiction, but it is also a story of redemption and the grace and love of God poured out on a broken man, attorney Nate O'Riley, whose personal and professional lives were in shambles. Alcoholism plagued him daily, drug abuse, two botched marriages, estranged children, four detox programs that didn't work, trouble with the IRS, and dengue fever. Hard, fast living had taken its toll. The weight of guilt over his past brought him to his knees in a little chapel hidden away in the streets of Corumbá, Brazil. He had come to the end of himself, which is where a person often finds the love of God patiently waiting with arms open wide to receive all who would come. "Sick, alone, broke, [and] under indictment,"[34] O'Riley wanted and needed forgiveness and a new start in life—a great need for a great God Who loves and cares for men just like him. Grisham described his dramatic transformation:

> *With both hands, he clenched the back of the pew in front of him. He repeated the list, mumbling softly every weakness and flaw and affliction and evil that plagued him. He confessed them all. In one long glorious acknowledgment of failure, he laid himself bare before God. He held nothing back. He unloaded enough burdens to crush any three men, and when he finally finished Nate had tears in his eyes. "I'm sorry," he whispered to God. "Please, help me."*
>
> *As quickly as the fever had left his body, he felt the baggage leave his soul. With one gentle brush of the hand [God's hand], his slate had been wiped clean. He breathed a massive sigh of relief....He wiped his cheeks and saw the face of Christ, in agony and pain, dying on the cross. Dying for him.*[35]

---

[34] John Grisham, *The Testament* (New York, NY: Dell Books, 1999). 360.
[35] *Ibid*, 374.

Such is the love of God that serves to remove yesterday's heavy "baggage" from one's soul, redeem what's left of our lives, and set us free to live life abundantly as God intended it to be lived.

Paul wrote to the church at Rome, *"But God* [I love those words], *shows and clearly proves His [own] love for us by the fact that while we were still sinners* [powerless and rebels], *Christ* [the Messiah, the Anointed One] *died for us"* (Romans 5:6, 8, 10, AMPC). The very essence of the love of God is found in and defined by two simple but powerful words repeated twice in verse 8: *"for us."* God's love *"for us,"* and again, God's sacrifice *"for us."* The point is this: the unfathomable, indescribable, indestructible love of God is invested *"for us,"* for our triumph in this life and the life to come.

Martin Luther once read the account of Abraham offering Isaac on the altar (Genesis 22) to his wife, Katie. She said, "I do not believe it [Sounds all too familiar]. God would not have treated his son like that!"

"But Katie," Luther replied, "He did."[36]

From eternity past and future, the words *"for us"* remains the emphasis of the divine plan forged in the heart of God. The cross has always been the focal point of the greatest love story of all time, and the Gospel is the greatest offer ever made to a wayward humanity.

When God's love and forgiveness is let loose upon the *"inner man,"* watch what happens. You cannot remain the same as you once were. It's impossible. *"Though our outward man is decaying, yet our inward man is renewed day by day"* (2 Corinthians 4:16-18). Divine love conquers all (1 Corinthians 13:8). The Gospel, the Good News of the grace and mercy of God, overwhelms and overpowers even the most disenchanted and hardened skeptic and the worst transgressors of decency and moral law. There is nothing you've

---

[36] Roland Herbert Bainton, *Here I Stand: A Life of Martin Luther,* Barakaldo Books. Kindle Edition, 466.

ever done to get God to love you. There is nothing you can do to get God to stop loving you. God cares. God loves, even the likes of you and me, and He wants us to succeed. He wants us to walk out the door each morning in *"newness of life"* (Romans 6:4, NASB) with our head lifted high, not dragging our knuckles through the dirt, discouraged and demoralized.

Chris Broussard is an internationally known sports analyst, commentator, and broadcaster for FOX Sports. He cohosts "First Things First" and appears regularly on FS1's *Undisputed* and *The Herd with Colin Cowherd.* In a recent podcast, he admitted:

> *I've been blessed to meet so many famous and incredible people, but meeting all of them combined has not given me a fraction of the joy, the peace, the value to my life that meeting Jesus Christ did on my 21st birthday... no matter what comes, I'm rooted and grounded, and I know I'm founded on Christ.*

Indeed, he is divinely favored, as we all can be and should be, living a life built on the love of God for us—a love that "endures long and is patient and kind," a love that "bears up under anything and everything that comes, is ever ready to believe the best of every person, a love that "never fails [never fades out or becomes obsolete or comes to an end]" (1 Corinthians 13:4-8, MSG). That's God's love for us.

God's love is bigger and better than anything you or I could ever conceive or imagine. His very nature is love. He defines love, a love dramatically different in every way than anything we've ever known. It is unique, wholly other, steadfast, unselfish, sacrificial, sustaining, dependable, and satisfying. Apart from God, the world of flesh and blood knows nothing of such things. If we're honest, our idea of love extends no further than a good pizza or a Coney hot dog smothered with onions, mustard, and a little chili, if you like. God's love is much different, much deeper.

Paul Brand, the medical doctor, who pioneered the treatment for leprosy (Hansen's Disease), served in India. Following the exam of a patient, Brand reached out and gently placed his hand on the shoulder of the sick man and explained the treatment for his medical condition. The man began sobbing. Brand asked, "Have I done something wrong?" A translator responded, "No, doctor. He says he is crying because you put your hand around his shoulder. Until you came here, no one had touched him for many years."[37]

The love of God is the touch of God, reaching down through the corridors of human history to the streets where you and I live, to rescue, redeem, and make whole the lives of people helplessly trapped in tragic circumstances, depressed, destitute, diseased, and spiritually bankrupt. The leper, who begged Jesus to make him whole (Matthew 8:3), was touched by the compassion and power of God. The eyesight of two blind men were restored. They cried for mercy (Matthew 9:27-29) and got it. Even the slave of the high priest who lost his ear in a fight with Peter in the Garden of Gethsemane (Luke 22:50-51) was made whole by the loving touch of God incarnate. On another occasion, Jesus reached out and *"took the hand"* of the daughter of a local official. She had died and her father was mourning her death. With a gentle touch, the Giver of life raised the girl from the dead (Matthew 9:23-25). *"Love,"* said John, *"is from God"* (1 John 4:7-11), the One who is forever touching the lives of people. *"O How He Loves You and Me."*[38]

Sixty years ago, Christian artist and writer, Bill Gaither, wrote (1963) the song, "He Touched Me,"[39] which captured the wonder of God's great love that changes lives for the better, brings hope wherever it goes, and heals the wounds of a soul left beaten, bruised, and bloodied along the road heading to Jericho. Ask the good Samaritan who exemplified God in action: *"And when he saw him,*

---

[37] Jeff Kennon, *The Cross-Shaped Life*, (Abilene, Texas: Leafwood Publishers, 2021), 97.
[38] Kurt Kaiser, *O How He Love You and Me*, 1975 Word Music, LLC.
[39] Bill Gaither, He Touched Me, 1963

he felt compassion…(and stopped), bandaged up his wounds…and took care of him" (Luke 10:25-37).

As a child, I often sang, *"Jesus loves me this I know, for the Bible tells me so."* Little did I know how deeply those words would impact my later life and future ministry. They are profound and powerful. *"Jesus loves me."* If He loves me (and He does) despite my long list of personal faults, frailties, and failures, He loves you, too. The potential ramifications and importance of those words for our lives cannot be overstated. No more crippling fears to unsettle my thinking or ruin my dreams. No more living like a victim. No more unwarranted worries to raise my blood pressure and kill my joy. No more self-pity. No more wasted years spinning my wheels and going nowhere fast. And no more open wounds that never heal, and so much more.

God's love covers it all and extends to the boundaries of eternity and beyond. It permeates and penetrates to the deepest corners and crevasses of the human heart, and in particular, to the core of my very soul and yours. Even today, after seventy-seven years of life on planet earth and more than fifty years of ministry behind me, I still cannot, nor will I ever, be able to fully grasp the depth of those words and adequately define and explain the wonder of God's matchless love and grace this side of eternity. I'm sure glad, however, and thankful to be on the receiving end of His care and concern. In his classic, *Mere Christianity*, C.S. Lewis reminds us:

> *The great thing to remember is that, though our feelings come and go, His love for us does not. It is not wearied by our sins or our indifference; and, therefore, it is quite relentless in its determination that we shall be cured of those sins, at whatever cost to us, at whatever cost to Him.*[40]

---

[40] C.S. Lewis, *Mere Christianity (1952)*, (New York, NY: Harper Collins, 2001), 132-133.

Love is always costly, and God's love *for us* cost Him plenty.

God is dedicated to your success and mine. The love of God unleashes the power of God to achieve the purpose and plan of God for your life. That's how it works. No surprise here. *"His banner over me is love"* (Song of Solomon 2:4, ESV).

Lysa TerKeurst, New York Times bestselling author and president of Proverbs 31 Ministries, has faced a number of tough challenges in her lifetime. As she describes it, it has been "one hardship after another." She could not wrap her mind around the magnitude and faithfulness of God's love, and asked God (as most of us have), "Why would You allow this to happen?" She suggested a different question:

> *As much as I want answers for those things that break my heart, I need to ask myself what I want and need most. Answers ... or Jesus?*
>
> *Let's be careful not to get stuck in our questions of why. "Why me? Why this?" Questions that can end up so consuming our thoughts that we become blind to His presence, blind to His goodness, blind to His power, blind to the hope we have in Him.*
>
> *I know this isn't easy. Trust me. I have situations where I've begged God to give me answers. But I'm realizing instead of answers, He's given me Himself...I don't have to have His answers to have His comfort.*[41]

Wise counsel to want Jesus...most of all. He holds the final answer to every question that comes to mind, particularly when tragedy strikes, and the pain is overwhelming.

In an earlier commentary on life's struggles, TerKeurst wrote:

---

[41] Lysa TerKeurst, Surrendering our 'Why' questions, *Proverbs 31 Ministries,* March 16, 2023, retrieved from https://proverbs31.org/read/devotions/full-post/2023/03/16/surrendering-our-why-questions.

> *I must process my hurt through the filter of God's love, not the tangled pieces of my heart. When I process things through my heart, the outcome is, 'If God loves me so much, why would He let this happen?' Instead, when I process things through the filter of God's love, the outcome is, 'God loves me so much, therefore, I can trust why He is allowing this to happen."*[42]

God's love remains unconditional for all time and eternity. This is the God Who:

> **Psalm 103:1-5, 8-11, MSG** – *Forgives your sins—everyone. He heals your diseases—everyone. He redeems you from hell—saves your life! He crowns you with love and mercy... He wraps you in goodness... He renews your youth... He makes everything come out right; he puts victims back on their feet. God is sheer mercy and grace; (He's) not easily angered, he's rich in love. He doesn't endlessly nag and scold, nor hold grudges forever. He doesn't treat us as our sins deserve, nor pay us back in full for our wrongs. As high as heaven is over the earth, so strong is his love to those who fear him.*

This is the God I can trust.

I was recently at a conference with social workers, medical staff, counselors, mental health professionals, law enforcement officers, local politicians, and members of the Salvation Army. They had gathered together to address the problem of sex trafficking in the community. They discussed the horrendous impact it has had on the lives of victims and families alike, who are often left broken in spirit, wounded souls, and suffering terribly. The physical, mental, emotional, and spiritual fallout is debilitating, to say the least. It cannot be overestimated.

---

[42] Lysa TerKeurst, If God Really Loved Me ... September 23, 2019, retrieved from https://lysaterkeurst.com/2019/09/23/if-god-really-loved-me/.

One of the conference speakers told of her own pain and personal struggles, having felt hopeless, alone, sad, depressed, even suicidal, and lost without purpose and meaning. She felt God was distant, and either unwilling (for some reason unknown to her) or unable to meet her at the point of her suffering and need. At least, that was what she thought and what she believed. It was a deep, dark place.

One Sunday morning, she forced herself to go to church. She admitted it was a difficult decision. Nevertheless, she went, unsure if it would make a difference. During the praise and worship, she had trouble raising her hands to recognized God and the part He had played in her life. She desperately wanted to connect with Him but couldn't find the inner strength and fortitude to do so. She needed Him. Emotionally, she was spent. Completely exhausted. Spiritually in the pits, a hole she couldn't climb out of. With difficulty, she managed to raise her hands to ear level. She tried hard to go further and give God His due but was too weak. She had gone as far as she could. The pain, agony, and uncertainty were too much to bear. She was in trouble.

A woman, who was sitting nearby, noticed her struggles. Sensing the depth of her agony, the woman left her seat and did the unthinkable. She did what Aaron and Hur did for Moses in the battle with the Amalekites when they *"held his hands up—one on one side, one on the other—so that his hands remained steady till sunset"* (Exodus 17:12, NIV). A stranger with the compassion of God walked behind that discouraged young soul, and placed her strong hands under each elbow and pushed her arms up high over her head and held them there for the remainder of the worship service.

It was a special moment, a tender moment, an extraordinary moment when God showed up to bring hope for a hopeless soul, a newfound strength to support a troubled woman, joy to the hapless, life to a person dying on the inside, and divine direction and guidance to one who had lost her way. "That's love," the session leader said with a smile. "That's the love of God at work in my life." It was God coming along side, giving power where there was none and the gift of faith to recover and walk in newness of life in Christ. *"For God so loved the world* [and you can put your name in there] *that He gave..."* He is forever doing just that, giving love *for us.*

Johnathan Edwards, who helped pave the way for the Great Awakening of the 1700s, remarked, "There is such love and such grace in the heart of God [that] if you understood the length and breadth and height and depth of it, you would never be discouraged."[43] An important insight for successful, daily living, a God Who gladly extends His loving, compassionate, nailed-pierced hands to embrace and lift you out of the muck and mire that's been weighing you down each day. That's "Good News."

Let me offer a final word of encouragement and exhortation from a dying man with little hope for his future. Diagnosed with ALS (Lou Gehrig's Disease), he said, *"Lose yourself in the wonder of God's love."*[44] Great advice, especially for my friend at the mall, who probably never heard the words, "I love you," in his entire life. But God was the first to say it and show it.

---

[43] Dane Ortlund, Jonathan Edwards on God's love for You, *The Gospel Coalition,* January 8, 2017, retrieved from https://www.thegospelcoalition.org/podcasts/word-of-the-week/jonathan-edwards-gods-love/

[44] Ed Dobson, *Seeing through the Fog,* (Colorado Springs, Colorado: David C. Cook, 2012), 110.

> *I have been asked hundreds of times in my life why God allows tragedy and suffering. I have to confess that I really do not know the answer totally, even to my own satisfaction. I have to accept, by faith, that God is sovereign, and He is a God of love and mercy and compassion in the midst of suffering.*
>
> –Billy Graham

CHAPTER 3

Why So Much Pain and Suffering in the World?

Pollster, George Barna, once questioned Americans, "If you could ask God one question and know that you would receive an answer, what would you ask?" Not surprisingly, the number one response was: "Why is there pain and suffering in the world?" C. S. Lewis remarked that the problem of suffering is atheism's greatest weapon against the Christian faith.[45] It's a question we must take seriously and attempt to answer.

In late March 2023, Rolling Fork, Mississippi, was hit by an EF-4 tornado, with winds of more than 166 MPH. The homes and businesses of an entire community were leveled to the ground, "leaving mounds of lumber, bricks and twisted metal." The winds even "ripped the steeple off" the local Baptist church.[46] The life once

---

[45] Ray Pritchard, Question for God, *Keep Believing Ministries*, August 16, 2014 , retrieved from https://www.keepbelieving.com/sermon/questions-for-god/#:~:text=Several%20years%20ago%20pollster%20George,on%20every%20hand%2C%20and%20we.

[46] Emily Wagster Pettus, Michael Goldberg and Rogelio Solis, 'There's nothing left': Deep South tornadoes kill 26, *Associated Press*, March 25, 2023, retrieved from

known by a community of people was over. There was nothing left, just a pile of rubble. To complicate matters, many of the town's people were without the financial and personal resources to recover from such a disaster. Thirty-five percent of the county residents lived below the poverty line and could not afford to rebuild after losing so much. Twenty-six people died that night when the storms hit the rural areas and more than half of those who died lived in Rolling Fork.[47]

One man, whose roof was torn off his home, said, "Yesterday was yesterday and that's gone – there's nothing I can do about it. Tomorrow is not here yet. You don't have any control over it, so here I am today." A local TV reporter, who saw the damage, prayed on live TV with great feeling, "Oh man, dear Jesus, please help them. Amen."[48] He saw people in great need and suffering terribly. The pain of such tragedy demands answers, especially from an all-powerful God Who says He is good and kind and yet does not appear so, given the results of the storm.

> *For the atheist, the basic argument goes like this:*
> *If God is all-good, He will destroy evil.*
> *If God is all-powerful, He can destroy evil.*
> *But evil is not destroyed.*
> *Therefore, there is no all-good, all-powerful God.*

For the theist, the argument may be summarized as follows:

> *If God is all-good, He will defeat evil.*
> *If God is all-powerful, He can defeat evil.*

---

https://apnews.com/article/tornado-texas-severe-weather-mississippi-valley-65e553e6358b56b2630ff5c588850505.

[47] Emily Wagster Pettus, Robert Bumsted And Rebecca Santana, Mississippi tornado victims wonder, 'How can we rebuild?' *Associate Press*, March 25, 2023, retrieved from https://apnews.com/article/mississippi-tornado-rolling-fork-silver-city-a61f1ee709ad81568d9ef410315d817a.

[48] Ibid.

> *Evil is not yet defeated.*
> *Therefore, evil will one day be defeated.*[49]

The problem of evil is both a personal and corporate moral issue. History is riddled with tragedy, including the most obvious: the record of human wickedness across all cultures and generations, malice, broken hearts, ruined marriages, banged up bodies, human atrocities, and self-destructive behavior, *"doing what we [feel] like doing, [and] when we [feel] like doing it"* (Ephesians 2:1-3, MSG). The human dilemma is well established and irrefutable. Examples of moral disasters are plentiful throughout world history.

The tribe of Judah had run out on God, thumbed their noses in the face of God (I've done that), and failed to obey God's commandments (done that, too), which were/are divinely designed and written for their/our well-being, safety, and health. The people of Judah lived as they pleased (like most of us do), unfaithful, obstinate, rebellious, and disobedient to the divine mandates. In short, the race of men and women want God out of the picture. The results of transgressing God's Word are predictable and catastrophic. There is no escaping the consequences of foolish decisions and reckless, riotous living (Ephesians 5:18). *"The wages of sin is death"* (Romans 6:23, NKJV), always, and remains operational (physically, emotionally, and spiritually) to this day. A person can die a thousand deaths before his/her feet ever hits the grave. We should stop blaming God. We've brought the judgment of God on ourselves. We have deliberately:

> *Drunk the cup of bitterness to its dregs, and have added weight to (our) sorrow... the result of (our) own impenitence and transgression. This is the bitterest of all—to know that suffering need not have been; that it has resulted from indiscretion and inconsistency; that it is the harvest of one's own sowing; that the vulture*

---

[49] Norman L. Geisler and Paul D. Feinberg, *Introduction to Philosophy: A Christian Perspective*, (Grand Rapids, Michigan: Baker Book House, 1980), 321.

> *which feeds on the vitals is a nestling of one's own rearing. Ah me! this is pain! There is an inevitable Nemesis in life. The laws of the heart and home, of the soul and human life… the awful pressure of pain; the trembling heart; the failing of eyes and pining of soul; the harp on the willows; the refusal of the lip to sing the Lord's song.*[50]

Very little has changed since the inception of mankind.

Isaiah saw *"the Lord sitting on a throne lofty and exalted"* (Isaiah 6:1, NASB), *"the King, the Lord of hosts" (v. 5)*, the God of all creation, unchallenged, unopposed, controlling, ordaining with all authority and power. Isaiah found himself in the presence of the majesty and splendor of almighty God. He had little to say except, *"Woe is me, for I am ruined"* (v. 5, NASB). No other words better reflect the state of humanity. It was all Isaiah could muster. The word *"ruined"* might also be rendered, *"silenced,"* or *"I'm as good as dead"* (v. 5, MSG). There are times when it's best to just keep our mouths shut and say nothing to justify that which is unjustifiable or excuse behavior that is inexcusable and indefensible. No excuses. I've screwed up.

Bill Parcels, former head NFL coach for the NY Giants, was told by his boss, George Young, following a dismal 3-12-1 season, that he was considering another coach for the following year. Parcels offered no defense or justification for the team's failure. He simply replied, "What can I say? You are what your record says you are."[51] And my record is not so good, either. Results speak for themselves in athletics and in life, anywhere where performance matters.

Evil also appears in the natural order of this world. In August 2023, a devastating fire raced through Maui with blinding speed.

---

[50] F.B. Meyer, *Christ in Isaiah*, (London, England: Morgan and Scott, Ltd, 1914), 9-10.
[51] Mike Vaccaro, The Giants' reality is absolutely ridiculous, *New York Post*, November 29, 2020, retrieved from https://nypost.com/2020/11/29/giants-defying-bill-parcells-mantra-in-most-ridiculous-way/.

Dry conditions and strong winds fueled the flames. There was no warning. Everything in its path was destroyed, homes flattened, businesses wiped out, churches burnt to the ground, people's lives wrecked...everything ruined. At last count, there were at least a hundred or more dead and that number is expected to rise. It is reportedly the deadliest US wildfire in more than a century. One man, Anthony Garcia, stood among the rubble which once was his home and surveyed the wreckage. He said, "I'm losing my faith in God."[52] How quick we are to fault God for the calamity in our lives. How slow we are to thank Him and recognize His goodness when things are going well.

Everything God did prior to creation and beyond was/is marked with these words: *"and God saw that it was good"* (Genesis 1:12, 1, 16, etc.). In fact, the creation account states that after surveying His own work, God Himself said, *"It was very [exceedingly, abundantly] good"* (Genesis 1:31). Not just good, but *"very good,"* exceptionally good, remarkably good...perfect in every way *good*. Nothing was or is overlooked in God's schemes. No stone was left unturned. All of creation stood in perfect harmony as a testimony to the goodness and perfection of God's decisions and actions. Tear back the curtain of God's purpose and plan, and you will find *good* (*tobh*), as in pleasant to the senses, gratifying, beneficial, beautiful, satisfying, the very best of qualities. Excellence, if you will, was the standard for God's creation from start to the finish seven days later.

We see glimpses of the beauty of God's artwork everywhere. He is the master Painter. *"The heavens declare the glory of God, and the sky above proclaims his handiwork"* (Psalm 19:1, ESV). It is how God has always worked. What God does cannot ever be improved upon. He does nothing half-heartedly. He leaves nothing

---

[52] The Associated Press, 'I'm losing my faith in God': Death toll rises to 80 in Maui wildfires as survivors begin returning to communities in ruins, Aug. 12, 2023, retrieved from SIlive.com/news/2023/08.

undone. He is at work in the world and in my particular life, and it's all good, whether I see it immediately or not, whether I understand it or not, whether I like it or not.

When God created the universe, He made it distinctly and functionally moral with the potential for men and women to do right and the potential to do wrong. He built into the world of humanity the ability to choose, to choose both good and/or to choose evil. It couldn't be any other way. That choice was/is necessary for a moral universe and free human beings to exist, to work and play, raise families, and live out their days.

So, what has happened in this world of woe? Genesis 3 and following happened: the fall of man. Adam and Eve chose to go their own way rather than God's. The results of such rebellion and poor decision making introduced evil and moral corruption and the consequences thereof into the cosmos. They opened the door to the cage, and death and hell raced out, seeking to sink their teeth into the hearts of its victims and devour them (1 Peter 5:8), leaving behind *"a valley of dead man's bones"* (Ezekiel 37:1). The results were the sure downfall of humanity, the rejection of truth and the reality of God, the long record of self-destruction, selfishness, self-centeredness, self-promotion, pride, deception, jealousy, hatred, rage, and more. It wasn't long after those early days of man's habitation on earth that Cain killed his brother in a jealous rage (Genesis 4:4-8), and the human race was off and running in the wrong direction, each man/woman seeking their own advancement at the expense of another, each one redefining reality to his/her own liking, each one rejecting absolute truth as the only standard to live by.

Sin and death brough in rust and decay, all manner of disease, and natural disasters, the likes of which strike fear in the hearts and minds of people across the planet, such as a tornado leveling a small town, hurricanes that flood a city and displace millions, a tsunami sweeping over a coastline, destroying property and drowning hundreds of unsuspecting people, locus swarming over fields of vegetation, leaving a portion of the world in famine, draught disrupting the cycle of planting and harvest, volcanic eruptions, and wildfires burning acres of forests and residences. You name it. All creation is under God's curse for our rebellious attitude and subsequent, spiteful actions (Romans 8:20-23, NLT). The universe has been summarily turned wrong-side-up and is *"groaning"* (Romans 8:20-23). You can't avoid it. You can't miss it. Suffering and tragedy abound, and we did it.

Edgar Allan Poe described his own experience with grief and loss in this world:

> *Deep into that darkness peering,*
> *long I stood there wondering, fearing,*
> *Doubting, dreaming dreams no*
> *mortals ever dared to dream before;*
> *But the silence was unbroken,*
> *and the stillness gave no token…*
> *Merely this, and nothing more.*

We are in trouble. The indictment has been *"written."* The charges read.

> **Romans 3:10-18, AMPC** – *None is righteous, just and truthful and upright and conscientious, no, not one. No one understands [no one intelligently discerns or comprehends]; no one seeks out God. All have turned aside; together they have gone wrong and have become unprofitable and worthless; no one does right, not even one…Destruction [as it dashes them to pieces] and misery mark their ways…There is no [reverential] fear of God before their eyes.*

The whole of mankind stands guilty for every mass casualty event, every pandemic, every plague ever set loose on the earth, for every crack-house, every bag of cocaine, every life lost to overdose, and every fentanyl pill manufactured and sold in our neighborhoods.

We are collectively answerable for every sickness known to man, for every abortion performed, every street gang which loots and runs rampant through the streets of our cities, every assault rifle fired inside the walls of an elementary school, for every DA across the nation who has swept criminal activity under the rug rather than cleaning it up, and so on. We may not have personally engaged in any such wrongdoing, but we stand complicit as a race before the court of God's tribunal, guilty of criminal conspiracy. All have sinned. All are lawbreakers. All are culpable. In the context of the judgement of God for *"deliberately continue sinning after we have received knowledge of the truth,"* (Hebrews 10:26, NLT), the writer of the epistle to the Hebrews warns, *"It is a terrible thing to fall into the hands of the living God"* (Hebrews 10:31, NLT). And so it is.

Theologian, R.C. Sproul, confirms the admonition:

> *He [God] is the Judge of heaven and earth, and He promises judgment; He will set the scales perfectly balanced. Now, we may complain that justice delayed is justice denied. But even in the delay, whatever injustice is found in there, God will redress. That is His promise to us...He has appointed a day, and though it seems slow,...(we) must wait for it, for "it will surely come" (Habakkuk 2:3).*[53]

I don't have all the answers, but I know this: prior to the Garden of Eden incident and the fall of humanity, Adam and Eve were in the best of situations, in a place made just for them, one that was tranquil, magnificent, more than adequate for their needs, pleasing, productive, and prosperous. There *"God planted a garden in Eden, (and) put the man he had just made in it. God made all kinds of trees grow from the ground, trees beautiful to look at and good to eat"* (Genesis 2:9, MSG). It must have been stunning to see and practical for the sustaining of life. They were set up for success,

---

[53] R.C, Sproul, *Why Is There Evil? (Crucial Questions)*, Ligonier Ministries, Kindle Edition, 51.

created by God *"in His image,"* and *"blessed"* by God to prosper (Genesis 1:27). In addition, they had been given a divine role to play and a job to do: to multiply, bear fruit, raise a family, cultivate the ground, govern as God's vassal kings and queens,[54] and rule the whole of nature to their advantage. The entire natural order was at their disposal to use for their own benefit and advancement. They were at peace with the world. That's how we started.

But things changed and not for the better. As representative heads of the human race, Adam and Eve rebelled against God and demanded their independence to live as they pleased apart from Him. They got what they wanted, and God let them go. In fact, they got more than they bargained for. The whole of nature and mankind itself came under the judgement of a holy God, and things went haywire. Shame and guilt emerged from the rubble, and with it came broken relationships with themselves, with God, and with the environment in which they lived. The ground was cursed. *"Thorns and thistles"* rose up to impede man's once promised success, and death entered the lives of people (Genesis 2:17), including the rest of creation, and all the universe suffered accordingly, and it still is. Cut yourself off from the God who gives life and everything around you will turn to *"dust...dead and buried."* That's where we are headed, the grave. *"You started out as dirt, you'll end up dirt"* (Genesis 3:8-9, MSG).

In conjunction with mankind's demise, the raw power of nature was consequently set loose *"to either punish people* [the recipients of God's judgement for our misdeeds and our transgressions of His law] *or to show his unfailing love* [mercy, forgiveness, and redemption] (Job 37:1-13). All creation is subject to His authority and power. All nature executes His commands (Psalm 148:8) and His righteous justice. The consequences of our cosmic rebellion are certain both morally and in the natural world.

---

[54] A vassal king is given land by another king in exchange for loyalty and allegiance.

Personally (like the whole of the human race), I have bought the Devil's lies and have heard his mocking laughter at my tears and brokenness. Consequently, I am compelled to fall prostrate before God, wounded and embarrassed, begging for mercy for the part I've played...for my wasted years, for my selfish behaviors, for every war ever fought, for nations rising up against nation, for neighbors battling neighbors, for ignoring the cry of those in need, for famine and pestilence, for judging a man by the color of his skin, for not speaking up to challenge the rise of foolish social values that smack in the face of common sense and human dignity and decency, and for human trafficking, slavery, drug and alcohol addictions, political scandals, suicide, and the like. The list of charges is long. The loss of common sense and a moral compass to guide human behavior is astounding. I need not look further. I am to blame.

A hundred years ago, William Butler Yeats, wrote a poem, entitled "The Second Coming." It details the condition of the world following World War I:

> *Turning and turning in the widening gyre*
> *The falcon cannot hear the falconer;*
> *Things fall apart; the centre cannot hold;*
> *Mere anarchy is loosed upon the world,*
> *The blood-dimmed tide is loosed, and everywhere*
> *The ceremony of innocence is drowned;*
> *The best lack all conviction, while the worst*
> *Are full of passionate intensity.*[55]

The world remains the same as in the past. Unless Christ comes to rectify the whole of Adam's race, and change the world, "the centre cannot hold." Humanity is doomed. *"Come, Lord Jesus"* (Revelation 22:20).

It's not a pretty picture, but it's true, the world lives by the motto of every man for himself. The evidence is overwhelming. The

---

[55] A. Norman Jeffares, *Poems of W.B. Yeats: A New Selection, Second Edition,* (Hampshire and London: MacMillian Education, LTD, 1988), 246-247.

world is a wreck, and so are the lives of its inhabitants. UN Secretary-General Antonio Guterres concluded, "We are gridlocked in colossal global dysfunction...These crises threaten the very future of humanity and the fate of our planet. Our world is in peril—and paralyzed."[56]

Admittedly, I have contributed to and am categorically responsible for the condition of a moral universe gone wrong and the consequential ruin of the natural world. God is not. We've done this to ourselves with the help and approval of hell, where evil plans its destructive and divisive strategy. Therein lies a partial answer for the magnitude and scale of the suffering and pain seen everywhere.

In the early 20th century, *The Times* of London sent out the following question to a number of politicians, philosophers, theologians, prominent authors, and social leaders. "What is wrong with the world today?" they asked. Among the many respondents, only Christian apologist, critic, and author, G.K. Chesterton, put his finger directly on the problem at hand. He simply wrote:

> *Dear Sir,*
> *I am.*
> *Yours, G.K. Chesterton*

In short, I am the problem. Dare I say, you are the problem, as well. We must not abdicate responsibility or deflect blame elsewhere. Better we own it. *"The foolishness of man undermines his way* [ruining whatever he undertakes]*; Then his heart is resentful and rages against the Lord* [for, being a fool, he blames the Lord instead of himself]" (Proverbs 17:3, AMP).

American comedian, Flip Wilson (1933-1998), used to say, "The devil made me do it." No, he did not. Within my own chest lies a dark, deceptive heart that is treacherous, *"desperately wicked"* (Jeremiah 17:9-10) and cannot be tamed. The American revivalist,

---

[56] David Rothkopf, As bad as the world looks right now, it's actually worse, *Daily Beast*, Sep. 23, 2022, retrieved from https://www.thedailybeast.com/as-bad-as-the-world-looks-right-now-its-actually-worse.

Johnathan Edwards, said unapologetically, "If God should open a window in the heart so that we might look into it, it would be the most loathsome spectacle that ever was set before our eyes."[57] None of us want to hear that or accept that as true about ourselves. It hurts.

Collectively, we've opened the door for evil to make its way into the world with devastating results, rooting itself in the soil of our souls, giving opportunity for evil to spread from generation to generation throughout all of God's creation and render people useless and ineffective in living out God's purpose and plan for our daily lives. *"When Adam sinned, sin entered the world. Adam's sin brought death, so death spread to everyone, for everyone sinned"* (Romans 5:12, NLT). We've given wickedness (*"iniquity" is* the biblical term) a foothold and access to the world we live in with our arrogance and self-will.

We have willingly and unwittingly submitted ourselves together to the unbridling of hell's rule and fury, and nature is no exception to the invasion of evil. William Lane Craig, a Christian apologist and author, wrote the following in his article, "The Absurdity of Life without God":

> *Modern man thought that when he had gotten rid of God, he had freed himself from all that repressed and stifled him. Instead, he discovered that in killing God, he had also killed himself. For if there is no God, then man's life becomes absurd" (meaningless, 'dark and terrible.'*[58]

A spiritual reset toward the good is required, and that is the focus of the Gospel message which carries the promise of a new life in Christ. *"Therefore, if anyone is in Christ, the new creation has come: The old has gone, the new is here!"* (2 Corinthians 5:17,

---

[57] Don Kister, ed, *Soli Deo Gloria*, 2002, From a collection of sermons by Jonathan Edwards, "The Wrath of Almighty God, " 9.

[58] William Lane Craig, The absurdity of Life without God, *Reasonable Faith*, retrieved from https://www.reasonablefaith.org/writings/popular-writings/existence-nature-of-god/the-absurdity-of-life-without-god.

NIV). Christ alone is the answer to the dilemma we face. We need a Savior. We need a *"living hope"* (1 Peter 1:3), *a "blessed hope"* as we wait for *"the appearing of the glory of our great God and Savior Jesus Christ"* (Titus 2:13, ESV). We need God. We need, as the song title states, the "Old Rugged Cross" for the forgiveness of our sins, and we must have the power of the resurrection of Christ to live like we should and replace evil with the best for our lives. God has not sat idle watching the world go to hell in a handbasket. Unless His love and grace intervene, the battle is lost, and suffering and pain will serve no particular meaning other than inflicting misery on the human race drowning in despair.

The New York Times bestselling author, Mitch Albom, runs an orphanage in Haiti. He has been there every month for the last twelve years or more as of this writing, helping out and supporting the work. He met a little girl, who had nothing, no family, no home, no future, nothing to call her own, and she was sick, suffering with a brain tumor. Her prognosis was not good. Albom and his wife adopted the little girl, whose name was Chica, and brought her to America in an effort to find a cure and get the medical treatment that potentially would save her life. They loved that little girl who stayed with the couple for two years and lived as their daughter. In the end, however, she died. There was no cure. Cancer eventually proved fatal. Albom said:

> *At the time, I was very angry at God...(but) wait a minute, she was born three days before an earthquake in Haiti. She survived the earthquake when a building fell down and around her, and she was three days in the rubble.*

She lived through that ordeal and survived two more years. And for what? To suffer and die anyway in the end? These are questions for God amidst great loss.

Today, Mitch has another perspective…and it comes out in his new novel, *A Stranger in the Lifeboat*. It's a story about a group of shipwrecked passengers, drifting along the open sea trying to survive. They were in trouble, nearing the end of their supplies when they spotted a stranger floating in the water. They grabbed him and pulled him into the boat.

"Thank the Lord we found you," said one of the passengers.

The man whispered, "I am the Lord…"

"What are you doing in the water?" asked another.

"Coming to you…Haven't you been calling Me?"

In the course of their conversation, God told them that He could save and rescue them, but first they all had to believe that he was God incarnate. The story unfolds around the dialogue between the stranger and the survivors regarding the issues of life, death, faith, and those questions that so often emerge when our lives have been shipwrecked.

Albom was being interviewed by Eric Metaxas about the questions raised by hurting people. Albom said:

> *When people die, we ask why did God take them? Maybe a better question might be, "Why did God give them to us in the first place? What did we do to deserve their love, their sweetness, their memories? Those memories are a gift. Their absence is not a punishment."*

In the book, God addressed the survivors who had lost everything of importance, particularly those they had loved:

> *"I'm not cruel," God said to them. "I knew you before you were born. I know you after you die. This earth you are on here, now, is just part of the journey. I know that you cry when your loved ones die and leave this earth. But I can assure you they are not crying."*

There are two ways to go here. Either we let the wave of despair and suffering come crashing down upon us and crush the life from us, or we ride the wave of faith and trust in the God of this universe and live. I know which way I'm leaning. Christianity has the best answers this side of eternity to explain the presence of pain and suffering so evident in this world, but nobody has got it all figured out, and I'm no exception to the rule. But Christianity will bring you a faith perspective and a bibliocentric viewpoint about life's sufferings...a perspective we can live with and a knowledge and awareness of God's presence and providence in the midst of hell on earth. Jeff Meyers, president of Summit Ministries, wrote in his book, *Understanding the Times*:

> *The Christian worldview offers a narrative of all history. This narrative starts with the special creation of human beings by God, delves into the consequence of their fall from grace, and promises redemption through the sacrificial death of Jesus on the cross and his subsequent resurrection.*[59]

"*Thy word is truth*" (John 17:17), said Jesus, the absolute, inerrant, infallible word of the living God upon which a man or woman can face all of life's ups and downs with the confidence and certainty that he/she has built a life worth living until death comes and eternity looms in the near distance.

Her name was Gail, a wonderful, delightful woman with a deep love relationship with God, a strong, seasoned Christian. Life hasn't always been easy. She battled cancer for many years. Twelve times, the dreaded disease returned, the last one with a vengeance. Many others with lesser fortitude and spiritual grit would have crumbled into a pile of self-pity, deep depression, and bewilderment a long time ago. Not her. She handled each setback with class, maintaining her faith, trusting God along the way, and exhibiting a

---

[59] Jeff Meyers and David A. Noebel, *Understanding the Times: A Survey of Competing Worldviews*, (Manitou Springs, Colarado: Summit Ministries, 2015 First Edition), 11.

joy and peace that cannot be explained other than by the presence of God in her daily life. Her prognosis was grim. The doctors gave her just months to live unless God steps in with a miracle.

She said, "The first time I got cancer twenty years ago, I told my husband that I don't want to sit around and whine," and she certainly hasn't done that. "I'm going to share this somehow for God's glory. I want Him to be glorified through this." She told two of the hospital staff, "I've had cancer twelve times and God has blessed me through it all." She told them how Jesus had helped her through all the chemo, multiple surgeries, and various radiation treatments.

Looking into the eyes of her attendants, she asked them the question of the ages, a question every person will someday have to answer. "Do you know Jesus?" Cancer had sapped her strength, but she remained focused and more concerned for the eternal well-being of the people around her than her own failing body.

John Wesley is credited with saying, "Our people die well." And when Gail was called home, she died well, too. She died well, because she had lived well, a life anchored to the "Rock of Ages," a life built on *"the way, the truth, and the life"* (John 14:6)…Jesus.

Carson-Newman University's legendary football coach, Ken Sparks, was dying of prostate cancer. He said to his son, "I've tried to teach you how to live *for Christ*. Now I want to show you how to die *with Christ*."[60] Gail did just that, as did Coach Sparks.

That morning outside the hospital, two hurting souls heard the Gospel message of God's love from the mouth of a small, fragile woman sitting in a wheelchair waiting for her ride home. Both individuals, who undoubtedly have suffered in this life, surrendered their lives to Christ, two precious people, who will never again be the same, are bound for glory. And Gail just sat there quietly and smiled, marveling at the wonder of the grace of God. Soon after, she

---

[60] Ciera Danielle, Sparks: The Ken Sparks Story, Double J Productions, January 7, 2022, retrieved from https://www.youtube.com/watch?v=kKF0olPg3hc.

met her Jesus and heard Him say, *"Well done, good and faithful servant"* (Matthew 25:21, NKJV). She showed us all, not only how to live *for* Christ, but also how to die *with* Him.[61]

Pain and sorrow are everywhere, but the "good news" is that better days are coming when tears will cease, and pain, discouragement, and hopelessness will be no more. God is making "Something Beautiful, Something Good,"[62] as the song title says, out of the brokenness and trouble in the world. A day will surely come when God will eventually and inevitably make things right once and for all and put the cosmos back in moral and natural working order. The suffering and the hurts you've endured, the injustices and prejudices you've borne, the disappointments you've shouldered, the tears you've shed, the doubts you've raised, the storms you've weathered, all of it and more will be put to flight. "What a day of rejoicing that will be."

In writing for *Christianity Today*, Kindra Sophia Soto, wrote of the pain she experienced from a displaced spine and her gratefulness for the subsequent healing that took place following surgery. She reminds us:

> *Living in a hurting body and a hurting world has caused me to witness how we as sinning, suffering children of God, often fail to see how God is present in the rubble and ruin of our lives. Even more so, we often forget that God is not only present there but longs to be present there—for and with us in our greatest distress...*
>
> *Our God is not only the One who heals. Our God is the One who stays. Holding onto this promise of His presence is key to suffering well (with God and one another)—most definitely, when our affliction lingers,*

---

[61] My Gospel Conversation, Red Bank Baptist Church, August 2023, Retrieved from http://vimeo.com/853016940.

[62] Bill and Gloria Gaither, *Something Beautiful, Something Good*, Gaither Music Co, 1971.

> *when our losses must be honored with tears, when all hope seems lost.*[63]

The person and presence of God in our pain and suffering, "*Immanuel...God with us,*" may be the greatest of all theological truths the world has ever seen and heard, for it holds the key to living victoriously amidst affliction and adversity.

---

[63] Kindra Sophia Soto, Suffering well when affliction lingers, *Christianity Today*, June 9, 2023, retrieved from https://www.christianitytoday.com/better-samaritan/2023/june/suffering-well-when-affliction-lingers.html.

Nothing whatever, whether great or small, can happen to a believer, without God's ordering and permission. There is no such thing as "chance," "luck," or "accident," in the Christian's journey through the world. All is arranged and appointed by God. And "all things" are working together for the believer's good.

J.C. Ryle (1816-1900),
first Anglican bishop of Liverpool, Church of England.

CHAPTER 4

How Is This Helping Me? What Purpose Does All This Pain Serve?

So often, I've not understood or (better yet) misunderstood God and His ways—which, I might add, are higher and better than mine. It's always been that way for every man and woman born into this world since the Garden of Eden. I simply don't get Him. My thoughts are not His thoughts, and neither are my decisions often His decisions. We should not be surprised by our spiritual ignorance nor the inability to grasp the fullness of God and His actions. In fact, His ways rarely correspond to my ideas or ideals of right and wrong, or my thoughts of good and evil, or what's of value and what's valueless. My evaluations of the events taking place in my personal life are all skewed toward my distorted, limited thinking. Frankly, I would do things differently than God.

Honestly, (I've said it before and will say it again), I've never, ever wholly understood the Godhead. Who does? Only God can *"explain"* God (John 1:18). Therefore, I remain intellectually stymied and spiritually stunted when it comes to God. Nothing new or surprising here. God lives and functions on a much higher plane than you and me (Isaiah 55:8-9). Consequently, I have made the mistake of misjudging or misinterpreting God's Word and actions. In fact, I've often pridefully resolved to pick a fight with heaven and quarrel with God over issues I know little about. Not a good move. The fact remains that I don't think like Him. I don't feel like Him. I don't see like Him. I don't behave like Him. And neither do you. Is it any wonder that we are quick to draw the wrong conclusions about Him, misjudge His intentions, and misalign His character. Only God can see and *"declare the end from the beginning"* (Isaiah 46:10). The psalmist wrote, *"How precious also are Your thoughts to me, O God! How vast is the sum of them! If I could count them, they would outnumber the sand"* (Psalm 139:17-18, AMP). I cannot wrap my mind around that.

I am reminded of the courtroom scene in the movie, *A Few Good Men* (Warner Brothers, 1992). The exchange between defense attorney, Lt. Daniel Kaffee (Tom Cruise) and Colonel Nathan Jessup (Jack Nicholson), the commanding officer at the time, is classic and insightful of human behavior and attitudes.

Kaffee demanded, "I want the truth!"

Jessup countered, "You can't handle the truth!"

The reality is neither can we, especially when questioning God and His decisions about the events He permits to invade our personal lives. Deep down, I want the truth, but can't "handle" it. Neither can I fully comprehend, nor am I able to understand, that which was planned in infinity and comes to pass in the finite world of men and women. No man or woman can do that.

Kobe Bryant, the "Black Mamba," played in the NBA for the Los Angeles Lakers from 1996 until 2016. In his tenure, Bryant won five NBA Championships, a 2008 Most Valuable Player, an All-Star for eighteen of his twenty seasons, a two-time NBA scoring champion, and was selected twelve times to the All-Defensive

Chapter 4: How Is this Helping Me? What Purpose Does All This Pain Serve?

team.[64] Bryant was considered one of the greatest players to ever lace up a pair of basketball sneakers. He unexpectedly died with his thirteen-year-old daughter, Gianna, and seven others in a helicopter crash on January 26, 2020. They were headed to his daughter's AAU basketball game. Bryant was forty-one.

The sports community was aghast. Fans from around the world were shocked. Who could explain such a thing? There seemed to be no consensus of opinion regarding this tragedy. The best Shaquille O'Neal, a former teammate of Bryant, could say was:

> *There are no words to express the pain I'm going through now with this tragic and sad moment of losing my friend, my brother, my partner in winning championships, my dude, and my homie. I love you brother and you will be missed.* [65]

Dwyane Wade, former player for the Miami Heat tweeted, "Noooooooooooo God, please no… It's like a bad dream that you just want to wake up from. It's a nightmare… Emotions are all over the place. These are the moments when you ask, 'Why?'"[66] Serena Winters, sideline reporter for the Cleveland Cavaliers said, "No way. I have no words. No words. Please tell me this isn't true."[67] The National Basketball Players Association (NBPA) released their official statement on the passing of Kobe. It read, "We are stunned and devastated…This is a monumental loss for the entire basketball community and our hearts are quite simply broken."[68]

---

[64] NBA Staff, Kobe Bryant: A basketball legend, *NBA*, February 25, 2020, retrieved from https://www.nba.com/kobe-bryant-tribute.

[65] Daniel Reyes, NBA Legend Kobe Bryant dies in a helicopter crash, *Mega Man*, January 27, 2020, retrieved from https://mega-onemega.com/nba-legend-kobe-bryant-dies-in-a-helicopter-crash/.

[66] Ryan Young, Dwyane Wade after Kobe Bryant's death: 'It's a nightmare,' *Yahoo Sports*, January 26, 2020,

[67] Hoops Hype, January 25, 2021, retrieved from https://hoopshype.com/2021/01/25/nba-twitter-the-day-kobe-bryant-died/.

[68] Spencer Kimball, 'Terrible,' 'heartbreaking,' 'devastated' — World leaders and athletes mourn the death of Kobe Bryant, *CNBC*, January 26 2020, retrieved from

67

From a human perspective, the entire tragedy seemed pointless. Fans and professional athletes alike were dismayed, speechless, distraught, in pain, brokenhearted, and in shock—the aftermath of human tragedy. There were no adequate explanations for the dire events that took place. Nobody could have imagined what would transpire that very morning, that the lives of nine people would end later that day. "No words" make sense. No rationale worthy of consideration. Nobody could see the divine purpose behind this tragedy. Sometimes, however, we do get a peek behind God's curtain and see a little bit of what He may be doing.

During the 2023 season, Damar Hamlin fell to the ground in the first quarter of an NFL game in Cincinnati. Cardiac arrest was the initial diagnosis. The stadium grew eerily quiet. As the players from both teams gathered to pray, the crowd watched the medical staff administer CPR twice and use a defibrillator to get the heart of a professional athlete started again. The heart attack came without warning. The situation was obviously serious, resulting in the game being rightfully postponed. After all, a young man's life hung in the balance. An ESPN sports reporter commented, "There are no answers." And answers (even the ones we don't want to hear) are what we feel we need and are entitled to receive. In fact, we demand it. We pound on God's chest and pull on His beard, insisting that He explain Himself. We want a rationale. We want a reason for all hell breaking loose in our lives, but we can't find one that fully satisfies our longing.

Another ESPN commentator and former NFL player, Dan Orlovsky, prayed unashamedly and boldly on live TV. Never have I witnessed anything like this before. God used these dire circumstances to gain the attention of the world. Orlovsky said, "It might not be the right thing to do, but it's on my heart. I'm going to

---

https://www.cnbc.com/2020/01/26/world-leaders-and-athletes-mourn-the-death-kobe-bryant.html.

bow my head right now and pray for Damar Hamlin." And so he did:

> *God we come to you in these moments we don't understand, that are hard, because we believe that you are God and that coming to you and praying to you have impact. We're sad. We're angry and we want answers, but some things are unanswerable. We just want to pray, truly come to you and pray for strength for Damar, for healing for Damar, for comfort for Damar – to be with his family, to give them peace. If we believed that prayer didn't work, we wouldn't ask this of you, God. I believe in prayer. We believe in prayer. We lift up Damar Hamlin's name in Your name. Amen.*[69]

In the midst of tragedy, God revealed Himself and arrested the attention of the world when He took hold of the life of a young, professional athlete who collapsed on a football field from a heart attack and in full view of national TV. In the chaotic moments that followed, God reminded us all of several great truths, just in case we had lost sight of what it means to be human.

1. **Life is precious.** It is to be revered, protected, and highly esteemed above all else. Nothing is of greater importance or value. Not money. Not fame. Not position or possessions. Not achievements or awards. Life is priceless. It is the greatest gift of all. When Hamlin awoke in his hospital bed, he asked, "Who won the game?" The doctors responded, "You did. You won the game of life." How right they were.

2. **There is a God.** He exists. He answers prayer. Prayer works. God is not deaf. His love and mercy are always accessible and available anytime, anywhere and is

---

[69] NFL Live (video), ESPN's Dan Orlovsky Praying for Damar Hamlin on NFL Live, *ESPN*, retrieved from https://www.youtube.com/watch?v=J1Vs59RDITc.

extended to those who would seek Him out to rescue, redeem, and to bring hope and courage in the face of the most severe circumstances.

3. **Have faith in God**, simply because faith connects us to the heavenly realm where we get our answers, gain our strength, and increase our hope in the midst of hopelessness.

4. **Nothing is impossible with God.** Eight days after his heart stopped, Hamlin was released from the hospital and showed up at the Buffalo Bills locker room to visit his teammates. One man remarked, "It's a miracle." God is still in the supernatural business.

5. **Life is not to be taken for granted.** You may not have tomorrow. You may not live to the end of the next hour or the next day. God reminded us all that we are mortal, and life can come to a screeching halt at any moment. Don't waste a minute.

6. **Life is short.** We don't have forever to do or be what we want or what we should. In those few moments, seen on our fifty-five-inch TV screens, we were reminded to live life to its fullest. Live with eternity in view. Remember, "It ain't over till the fat lady sings,"[70] and the "fat lady's" song, I will remind you, will be over before you know it. Who could have guessed what God was up to in the life of Damar Hamlin? Certainly not me.

More often than not, answers and understanding remain in short supply. What we do know is that pain and confusion are commonplace in a fallen world where the unexpected and the hurting take place seemingly without rhyme or reason. Nothing

---

[70] The phrase first appeared in the Dallas Morning News, 1976.

seems to make sense, especially when bad things happen to good people.

Often, the name of God is invoked in moments of tragedy, as we instinctively look for help from the only One we know able to effectively bring about change, healing, and peace of heart and mind (Philippians 4:7). In a time of great need, a great God can make a great difference in your life.

Unfortunately, however, God is blamed and found guilty of divine negligence in the courts of human opinion well before all the "evidence" is in. God could have prevented it (so goes the reasoning) but chose not to interfere for some unknown purpose beyond our knowledge. The Apostle Paul raises a direct question whenever we disapprove of God's decisions. *"Who are you, O man (or woman), who answers back to God?"* (Romans 9:20). A pointed question that disrupts our thinking. I suspect that the real, down-to-earth answers for which we oftentimes have no immediate understanding are concealed in the heart and mind of God somewhere in eternity past, present, and future.

Someday, all will be revealed, and we will finally catch a much better glimpse of who God is and what He is about. It is still true. God brings *"good"* amidst the most horrendous of circumstances and chaos, a tough lesson for anybody to learn and accept. In the meantime, we continue to struggle with setbacks and adversity in daily life. We know only this for certain: God is able to redeem any situation we may find ourselves in no matter how bad or hopeless it may seem and bring about His best for your life and mine.

Joseph is a prime example. Hated by his brothers, the boy was sold into slavery and ended up a servant in the house of Potiphar, *"an Egyptian officer of Pharaoh, the captain of the bodyguard"* (Genesis 39:1). Joseph was *"successful"* and advanced to *"overseer"* of the house. It was evident from the beginning that *"the Lord was with him"* (Genesis 39:3).

But things went wrong. He was falsely accused of sexual misconduct by Potiphar's wife and was arrested and imprisoned for something he didn't do. At no time, through all the ups and downs of Joseph's personal life, had God ever taken His hand or His eye off Joseph. In fact, God was orchestrating the details of his career. He had a plan much bigger than anything Joseph could have ever imagined. From a young age, he was being divinely groomed, equipped, and prepared to lead Egypt through a great famine and to eventually save the lives of his brothers who had betrayed him.

How do you explain a slave bound to an earthly master and rises above his station in life? Can you figure out how an innocent man falsely accused, facing a prison sentence and/or possible execution for a crime he didn't commit, rises up out of the ashes to become the second most powerful man in all of Egypt? Blind luck? Fate? The alignment of the stars? Palm reading? Or was it the working out of an outrageous, supernatural, divine plan? I think the only reasonable option is God.

Who could have known? Talk about a rags-to-riches story. Who could have written that script other than God? No one. Joseph eventually figured it out. He took stock of his life. He had been a little, obnoxious runt tied up and thrown into a pit by his own family to shut him up, sold as a slave, served time in a prison cell, and ended up walking the palaces of Egypt as an advisor to the throne, second in command over all of Egypt. He had seen firsthand the work of God. The proof was unmistakable. It could not be ignored or dismissed as happenstance. It was God from start to finish. Joseph could draw but one conclusion, *"Don't be afraid* [that rings true for all going through trial and suffering]...*Even though you intended to hurt me, God intended it for good. It was his plan all along, to ensure the survival of many people"* (Genesis 50:20, TPT).

God is and remains a mystery. He defies being put into a theological box for human consumption or manipulation and doctrinal convenience. *Incomprehensible* is the word theologians use to describe what little we know about the Creator of the universe, Who is *"before all things, and in Him all things hold together"* (Colossians 1:17). Let that rattle around in your brain for just a bit.

Words are obviously insufficient to explain the depths of divinity. Language is inadequate. Culture is of no help. The ideas of philosophers are no better. Reason is of little use here, especially when attempting to define and understand the Godhead (and that includes His decisions and actions). Good luck with trying to unscramble that.

Not surprisingly, we find ourselves hard-pressed to figure out God. I've tried. It doesn't work so well. My best efforts have left me dissatisfied, confused, and wondering at times if God is just too far away for me to get a good, unobstructed view of Him, too distant for me to connect with, and/or too mysterious for me to intellectually untangle or make sense of. The Bishop of Alexandria, St. Athanasius (296-373 AD), concluded, "For of what use is existence to the creature (me and you), if (me and you) cannot know (our) Maker."[71]

Finite beings are short on grasping infinity. What we think of God remains clouded in ambiguity and encased within our own self-serving ideas and often thoughtless opinions. Simply put, we have no accurate definitions of the divine nor do we possess a clear, unobstructed, complete understanding or view of who He is in His fullness, where to find Him, what He is up to, and what He truly desires from us all. Humanity has always surrounded itself with a plethora of gods, none of whom makes much sense to those who are searching for real answers and the God who can give clarity.

Zophar the Naamathite challenged Job, who was trying to understand his own troubles and where God might fit into the picture. *"Can you discover the depths of God? Can you discover the limits of the Almighty?"* he asked (Job 11:7). The questions are

---

[71] St. Athanasius, O*n the Incarnation: de Incarnatione Verbi Dei*, kindle edition, (C.R. Draper, Createspace Publishing, 2017), 22.

rhetorical. They demand a firm, "No, I can't!" *"The thunder of (God's) mighty power"* (Job 26:14) is beyond human comprehension. In fact, it strikes fear in each of us. It should. It is but a hint of God's omnipotence. The best Elihu (another of Job's friends with a big mouth) could say was that he *"fetched (his) knowledge (of God) from afar"* (Job 36:3). And *"afar"* is an accurate depiction of our inadequacies and theological shortsightedness. Elihu spoke the truth. The extent of our collective knowledge about God and God's ways are not terribly impressive. *"God is exalted, and we do not know Him"* (Job 36:26). But we need to, and we must come to terms with what God wants.

And this is certainly true when questioning God and the purpose behind His sometimes encouraging or uncomfortable decisions about the events He allows to invade our personal space. We want a sure word from God but continue to struggle with understanding the depth of God's specific decisions and actions. God's infinite plans unfolding in a finite world is always a source of trouble for flesh and blood. We're just not sure what to make of God at the helm. Yet, there is divine purpose, and therefore meaning in everything God does and allows. Sometimes His actions are shrouded in mystery, but there is a purpose nonetheless, even *When Bad Things Happen to Good People,*[72] as a book title so eloquently put it.

There is purpose in every act of God. There is purpose in the mundane affairs of daily life. God has purpose in a life lived in the heat of a barren desert, purpose in the lowest valleys of depression and disappointment, purpose in the highest peaks of achievement. There is purpose in the battles I must fight, no matter how big the giants. There is purpose in the victories I win and in the defeats I am called upon to endure. There is divine purpose in the ups and the downs of ordinary life, in my sickness, in my health, in my poverty and in my wealth, in my sorrows and in my fears. There is purpose

---

[72] Book title by Rabbi Harold S. Kushner, Anchor Publishers, 2004.

in my broken heart, and purpose in my joy. Every bit of it serves God's desires for my life, which is to glorify Him and to conform me in every way to the *"image of His Son"* (Romans 8:29). It is toward that lofty goal I must ultimately move. Rick Warren reminds us, "We were made by God and for God," and nothing in this life will ever make sense until we understand, accept, and apply that truth for our personal lives.[73]

---

[73] Rick Warren, *AZ Quotes, Facebook post by Pastor Rick Warren from Jan 04, 2013*, retrieved from https://www.azquotes.com/quote/307471?ref=purpose-of-god.

Are You (God) sadistic? Why do You leave me alive, God? Stop toying with me and just take me. I don't know what death is, but it can't be worse than this.... O God, I can't be this way, can't go on this way. How do I stop this long slide into nothingness?... So what's it all about, God, or... whoever You are? Do You bring people into this world just to breathe, eat, grow old, and die? Do You toss the dice and paralyze people along the way? Or throw in a little cancer ... a little Down syndrome ... or maybe smash someone's brains in an accident? Well? Tell me....[74]

–Joni Eareckson Tada, November 1967, University of Maryland Hospital, following an accident that left her a quadriplegic.

CHAPTER 5

How Could You Let This Happen?

It was mid-week. A troubled co-ed sat in my office with tears streaming down her cheeks, pleading for God's help and wondering why He had not in fact stepped in to rescue her. She was distraught over what had transpired in her early life and felt buried in debilitating depression, a victim of abuse at a church pre-school. Evil had taken it's awful, destructive toll on a three-year-old girl. Now, sixteen or seventeen years later, she is paying for hell's attempt to *"steal, kill, and destroy"* (John 10:10) her very life. I made little headway. She had already attempted suicide three to four times, and I was worried and angry with God that He seemed unaware of her sufferings (Exodus 3:7), or worse yet, seemed unable or unwilling to rescue her. At least that was how I felt. We talked for a while. I tried to encourage her as best I could, but to no avail.

She needed a miracle, a supernatural work of God to do what she obviously could not do for herself, bring healing and wholeness

---

[74] James Lau, The Anger That Heals by Joni Eareckson Tada, *My Inward Journey,* November 5, 2020, retrieved from https://jameslau88.com/2020/05/10/the-anger-that-heals-by-joni-eareckson-tada/.

to her life *"to the praise of His glory"* (Ephesians 1:14). Consequently, she desperately needed God to show up and lend a hand. In the course of our conversation, she hung her head and said in a soft voice, "I want to live, but God has got to help me. I cannot do this alone." Nobody can.

She left the building and headed to a counselor off campus. I hoped and longed for her to get some answers and find much needed relief. I wept and wanted to help in any way I could. So, I prayed. I had nothing else to offer. I laid my heart bare before the throne of God and tried to connect with Him on a much deeper level than previously experienced. I prayed in earnest with a newfound fervency. In retrospect, it may have been the best prayer I've ever attempted. It was honest, direct and clear, and it came in the form of a question. My eyes turned heavenward as I stood in my office, and I asked, "What kind of a God are You who can hear such a plea and turn a deaf ear?"

I wasn't sure I had reached heaven. I wasn't sure it would do any good. Essentially, I was shaking my fist in the face of God even before I had my answer from above. I was so angry I could have spit nails. I see it now—I didn't then—as an outright attack on God's character and His decisions. I spoke to Him as if He were an enemy out to get me, someone I detested or couldn't count on. Subsequently, I issued an ultimatum, a threat (something that doesn't ever work well with God), just in case He opted to move in a different direction than I would have liked. God had better do what I wanted, get in line with my ideals, and fast, or I'd be done with Him. No more. Write Him off. I've had enough of God screwing up my life.

God asked Jonah, "'Do you have a good reason to be angry about [the loss of] the plant?' And he [Jonah] responded, 'I have a [very] good reason to be angry, angry enough to die!'" (Jonah 4:9, AMP). I understand Jonah's fury, wanting the Ninevites to get what was coming to them for their treatment of the Jews, and I get his anger at God for potentially letting them off the hook. Jonah loathed them and was defiant toward God. What he didn't understand (and neither do I) is the grace and mercy of God. Jonah wanted retribution and revenge. God wanted to forgive, to redeem, and to save, and for that (the goodness and compassion of God) Jonah got mad at heaven for sparing a wicked people he thought warranted annihilation. God sees things much differently than we do. Jonah had no "good reason" to be mad. He was just plain angry, but not surprised by God's decisions.

C.S. Lewis looked back at himself as a 15-year-old boy trying to live with a surplus of intellectual and emotional conflicts. He said:

> *I was at this time living, like so many Atheists or Antitheists, in a whirl of contradictions. I maintained that God did not exist. I was also very angry with God for not existing. I was equally angry with Him for creating a world.*[75]

Anger at God is a battle no one has ever, nor will they ever, win.

Tim Keller wrote in his classic, *The Reasons for God*:

> *If you have a God great and transcendent enough to be mad at because he hasn't stopped evil and suffering in the world, then you have (at the same moment) a God great and transcendent enough to have good reasons for allowing it to continue that you can't know. Indeed, you can't have it both ways."*[76]

Ashamedly, I've been angry with God and guilty of doing what the Israelites had done in the desert thousands of years ago, *"grumbling against* [Him]*"* (Numbers 14:27), protesting, griping for no apparent reason, objecting, and faulting Him for my

---

[75] Peter Somervell, Angry at God for not existing, Peter Somervell Blog, November 25, 2016, retrieved from https://petersomervell.wordpress.com/2016/11/25/angry-at-god-for-not-existing/.
[76] Tim Keller, *The Reasons for God*, (New York, New York: Penguin Group, 2008), 25.

circumstances and the pain I was sure He was causing me. In essence, I have charged God with failing to take appropriate action as I see fit and accusing Him of not doing right or acting in a manner without my approval. I have the right to be angry, or so I've often thought. The audacity of such a thing. The height of arrogance. *"Who in the world do you think you are to second-guess God?"* asked the Apostle Paul, *"Do you for one moment suppose any of us knows enough to call God into question?"* (Romans 9:20, MSG). Apparently, I did, and sometimes, I still do with little to no results. Somebody once said, "Anger is a condition where the tongue works faster than the mind." All too true. I have a fast and lethal tongue.

Nothing has changed since men and women have walked the earth. We always seem (or pretend) to know more and better than God, or at least we act and speak like we do. The historical record shows that God used the word "evil" (Hebrew – *ra'*) to label Israel's disfavor of His plans, their incessant complaining, impatience, hostility, and impertinence. That's a strong word, which caught me off guard when I first read it.

The word "evil" in this context means to defame, to damage the reputation of another, to speak falsehood, to murmur against, and to promote or indulge in immorality and moral corruption.[77] Too often, God is on the receiving end of some sharp words that have no substance in reality. The character assassination of God before the world is a serious indictment, and I am guilty, as I stand before you embarrassed with head bowed low in great need of repentance and forgiveness in the judgement halls of the Almighty. Self-will is ugly and egotistical. We would do well to remember that when approaching God *"the place on which you [we] are standing is holy ground"* (Exodus 3:5).

In 1921, David and Svea Flood, along with two others (Joel and Bertha Erikson), hacked their way through thick jungle brush to

---

[77] The Lockman Foundation, Hebrew-Aramaic Dictionary of the New American Standard Exhaustive Concordance, (La Habra, California: Lockman.org, 1998).

establish contact with the indigenous tribes of the Congo. Their task, "if they chose to accept it" (sounds like a *Mission Impossible* adventure), was to bring the Gospel to people who had never heard the good news of God's amazing love and grace. The journey into the back country was hard and tough going, testing their faith and mettle with every step they took. Nothing came easy. Both families came down with malaria during their trek across the land.

First contact was finally made with the tribesmen, but neither couple were allowed to enter the villages. The chief feared that his gods would be offended. The two families were forced to build two mud huts in the middle of the jungle to survive the harsh conditions and to begin the work they had been sent by God to do. Malnutrition, loneliness, and sickness set in, and no advance of the Gospel was realized. Little was accomplished. Little to show for their efforts in six months of work. Joel and Bertha Erickson finally had enough and left the field to return to the base mission.

Svea Flood couldn't travel. She was pregnant and once again came down with a bad case of malaria. She eventually delivered a healthy baby girl, Aina, but Seva died from medical complications soon afterwards. David Flood was distraught, enraged, and bitter by what heaven had allowed to take place. He held God in contempt and personally responsible. *"Why did you allow this, God?"* he asked. *"We came here to give our lives! My wife was so beautiful, so talented. And here she lies, dead at twenty-seven."* A broken man, angry at God, he buried his wife and took his son back to the states. He left his daughter to be raised by the Ericksons in the Congo. His rage and disappointment drove him from ministry and from the Lord, and he lived out the remainder of his life as a drunk, sickly and angry at God. But the story doesn't end there.

Aina, Flood's daughter, who later became known as Aggie, gave her life to Christ, attended a Bible college, got married, and began serving the Lord. Some years later, Aggie and her husband attended an evangelism conference in London. A report was given from the Congo. The superintendent of the national church spoke eloquently of the Gospel's spread in his nation. There were now one hundred and ten thousand Christians, thirty-two mission stations, several Bible schools and a one hundred and twenty bed hospital. Following the report, Aggie asked the church leader if he had ever heard of David and Svea Flood. The man replied in French, "Yes, madam, it was Svea Flood who led me to Jesus Christ."

God had a plan. From one seed, He multiplied a great harvest. Anger robbed a man of the privilege of participating in God's grace and mercy and making a difference in the world. All those wasted years of bitterness. Shortly before his death, David Flood returned to the faith. He was reunited with his daughter who told him how God took the conversion of one small boy and the death of his wife and built a national ministry. Nothing God does is ever in vain.

Ray Stedman, who authored the classic, *Authentic Christianity*, wrote a parody of the Doxology. The words epitomized the views of many, especially when life goes south.

> *Blame God from whom all cyclones blow.*
> *Blame Him all creatures below.*
> *Blame Him who knocks down church and steeple,*
> *Who sends the flood and drowns the people.*[78]

Amusing, but tragic.

In January 2015 in an interview on Irish TV, Stephen Fry, British actor and atheist, criticized God for creating the world rampant with suffering (i.e. disease, famine, poverty, natural disasters, cancer, mental illness, wars, hatred, prejudice, death, etc.), none of which he believed is compatible and consistent with an all-powerful, loving, righteous, holy God who seems to tolerate the presence of evil in the world. Consequently, Fry referred to God as

---

[78] Ray C. Stedman, The Test, *Ray Stedman Authentic Christianity*, September 04, 1977, retrieved from https://www.raystedman.org/old-testament/job/the-test

an "utter maniac, utterly monstrous/evil, and totally selfish."[79] Harsh words laced with distain and anger. On another occasion Fry argued, "You can't just say there is a God because well, the world is beautiful. You have to account for bone cancer in children."[80] The problem is critical and demands an answer, though no man or woman has full comprehension at his or her disposal, including Stephen Fry. No one has it figured out on either side of the aisle, leaving us all frustrated and downright angry over the prevalence of evil, human suffering, and pain. Theologian, R.C. Sproul, reminded us that "The origin of evil has been called the Achilles' heel of Christianity…and Christians fail to feel the weight of the problem."[81]

The best minds the world has ever seen (from Plato, Aristotle, Archimedes of Syracuse, Augustine, Galileo, da Vinci, Newton, Einstein, Stephen Hawking, etc.) are baffled when considering the existence of God, who sits enthroned over the entire known and unknown universe, including a troubled world in which humankind breathes, lives, and dies. No one is able to see what God sees or know what God knows—past, present, and future, including the boundaries of eternity where time is no more. I cannot see beyond the end of my theological nose, or make sense of painful, unexpected circumstances, or plan my future from *"everlasting to everlasting"* with any degree of certainty (Psalm 103:8, 17). God's *"understanding is immeasurable"* (Psalm 147:5). Mine is not.

With a little humor, a Nevada elementary school teacher expressed her inability to grasp the intricacies of creation and its Creator. "When I die and go to heaven," she said, " the first question

---

[79] Stephen Fry quotations and quotes on God & Creationism, retrieved from https://www.age-of-the-sage.org/quotations/quotes/stephen_fry_gods_religions_beliefs.html.
[80] *Ibid*, The Importance of Unbelief. Interview on bigthink.com - recorded December 8, 2009.
[81] R.C. Sproul, *Why is There Evil*, (Sanford, Florida: Legionaire Ministries, 2021), 24 (Kindle).

I'm going to ask God is: 'Why did you create lice? What was that all about?'"[82] I think there are greater issues to consider.

Learning to live/walk by faith amid the mysteries of life so ordered by God might be a better approach, to trust Him more fully in each and every confusing and troublesome situation that comes our way, including lice. He is after all *"the only wise God our Savior"* (Jude 25). Paul wrote, *"Don't use your anger as fuel for revenge. And don't stay angry. Don't go to bed angry. Don't give the Devil that kind of foothold in your life"* (Ephesians 4:26-27, MSG). The application is to human relationships but can be applied to a healthy relationship with God.

There's a huge difference between weeping with a broken heart filled with pain and unanswered questions aimed at God about the harsh and unexpected trials. It's one thing to tell God how badly I hurt, how disappointed I am, how sorrowful I am, how confused I am. It is quite another matter to pick a fight with God. That's a fight you can't possibly win.

It's never acceptable to profess and possess a defiant, insolent attitude of rebellion and insurgency, raging against God, fists clinched heavenward, ready to duke it out with the Almighty. Threatening and trying to coerce Him into submission, fighting Him for supremacy, and standing up defiantly against His throne and rulership is unacceptable and self-destructive. Each time I radically and ruthlessly challenge God's rightful place as Lord over my affairs, I assist the demons of Hell, whose single purpose is to destroy my relationship with God, with others, and with myself.

There is a better way. Pour out your frustrations, your deepest pain openly and honestly to the One who is called *"a Man of sorrows and pain and acquainted with grief"* (Isaiah 53:3, AMP). God knows. He understands.

---

[82] John M. Glionna, More Lenient Rules On Head Lice Have Some Schools Jumpy, *Los Angeles Times*, Dec. 15, 2013, retrieved from https://www.latimes.com/nation/la-na-nevada-head-lice-20131216-story.html.

The opening few chapters of the book of Job clearly shows just how cruel, vicious, and devious the devil is, how he hated Job (including you and me) and all of God's creation, how he brought the hammer down on God's man again and again and again, how he broke Job's heart, crushed his spirit, and stole from Job everything that mattered, cared about, and was of great personal value. He unleashed hell's fury without mercy on a man innocent of wrongdoing. Satan's tactic was simple: utterly ruin and methodically destroy everything the man loved, and in the process, discredit God as the great Provider, Protector, and Promise-keeper. The devil held nothing back. Everything was on the table except killing the man, and Job lost all. No wealth. No possessions. No health. And ten fresh graves outside his tents. *"Through all this,* we are told, *"Job did not sin or did he blame God"* (Job 1:22). He maintained the integrity of his faith. Remarkable grit and strength of character. I could use some of that.

Job's wife, however, had another take on the matter. She saw and felt the loss deeply. She saw her husband's physical deterioration and weakened condition, a *"body covered with maggots and scabs...*[his] *skin...oozing with pus"* (Job 7:5, NLT). She saw his anguish and the depth of his grief over the death of his children and servants. She saw Job's life falling apart piece-by-piece, brick-by-brick till there was nothing left, and she was ticked at God, pointing an accusing finger. She held Him personally responsible and accountable. *"Curse God and die"* (Job 2:9), she screamed. Be done with God! It was the first time and the only time she spoke in Job's story.

I met David Biebel many years ago when he came to speak at the church I pastored in upstate New York. I remember him to be a quiet, gracious, and humble man who had lived through a nightmare. He has written two powerful books detailing the excruciating pain that so often accompanies great, personal loss. I devoured them both cover to cover.

The first book, *Jonathan, You Died Too Soon,* chronicled the death of David's three-year-old son and the emotional and spiritual journey through the dreadful experience of burying his youngest child. I can't even imagine the horror of it all. Jonathan died of an undiagnosed condition that took his life and his future. The book is a brutally honest account of personal grief, severe depression, and debilitating confusion, doubts, and fears.

The sequel to that book is entitled, *If God Is So Good, Why Do I Hurt So Bad?* The story is equally compelling and powerful. David's second son, Christopher, was struck with the same rare, genetic disorder that killed his brother, Jonathan. His father remembered the day he got the news from the medical staff. The prospects of yet another loss was devastating. Overcome with remorse, David watched helplessly the life of yet another child slip away. The hurt was all too familiar. Death was knocking at the door again. I cannot grasp such anguish, the loss of all hope, and the anger directed toward heaven. He was furious with God. Enraged might be a better word, livid, incensed beyond description and consolation. It was how David felt. No trite words, just the raw truth. No excuses, just questions. No Pollyanna Christianity, just reality. David wrote:

> *I look into the Father's eyes*
> *And wrestle with a thousand 'Whys'*
> *Why this? Why now? Why him, not I?*
> *Why us, not them? I can't disguise*
> *The hurt, the rage, unbridled pain*
> *Erupting from my soul, again.*
> *If that's the way it's going to be*
> *Then build Your kingdom without me.*[83]

---

[83] David C. Biebel, *If God is So Good, Why Do I Hurt So Bad*, (Colorado Springs, Colorado: Navpress, 1989), 146.

Chapter 5: How Could You Let This Happen?

How incredibly honest. He admitted, *"I don't think I can forgive God for this."*[84] I would have struggled with the same malady.

In the hospital, a broken, desperate man, a father with a wounded, hurting heart, hung his head and cried out in anguish and anger, *"If that's the way it is going to be, then God can go to...."* Yes. The man hurt that badly.

He reasoned, *"Isn't once enough? But twice? How can I serve a God like that? How can I love a God like that?"*[85] David decided to leave the ministry, questioning the very character of the God he once served and thought he knew and loved.

But God was not done. On the way home from the hospital, David got his answer. He recorded that experience:

> *Suddenly, as I drove, I realized that God had already gone to hell in the person of Jesus. And I knew that He had done so with a purpose, to redeem this sinful world - which allowed the possibility of genetic illness...and to redeem this sinful man, me...I have a living hope.*

Subsequently, Christopher survived and fully recovered. God intervened and was merciful, transforming David's anger and doubts "into a revelation of His redemptive love."[86]

The key to ridding ourselves of anger directed at God is twofold: First, get to know God better and deepen your relationship with Him prior to your world falling apart. You will find Him to be sharper and wiser than you ever thought, more capable, open, caring, and more loving and understanding than you could ever imagine. God knows what it's like to suffer the loss of a child. He must have cried at the sight of His only Son bruised, broken, and bleeding. The personal pain must have been excruciating, while watching and

---

[84] *Ibid*, 58.
[85] *Ibid*, 19-20.
[86] *Ibid*, 77.

knowing all the time that He could have stopped it but chose otherwise. *"There is no greater love than this—that a man should lay down his life for his friends. You are my friends if you do what I tell you to do"* (John 15:13-14, PHILLIPS).

The Apostle Paul advised believers:

> **Philippians 4:6-7, MSG** – *Shape your worries* [frustrations and anger] *into prayers, letting God know* [as if He didn't already know] *your concerns. Before you know it, a sense of God's wholeness, everything coming together for good, will come and settle you down.*

We have a tendency to focus on our problems, especially when they hit and hit hard. We look to find answers to the age-old questions surrounding the existence of a good, loving God and the suffering we so readily see and experience in this world. Better we see life as best we can from God's perspective, through His eyes, rather than looking for God in the troublesome events and problems that touch our lives and blinds us to the reality and character of God.[87] When you focus on Him, the peace of God will *"guard your hearts and minds"* (NASB). *"The Lord* [becomes and feels] *near"* (Philippians 4:5, NASB), softening every spiteful, hateful, and stubborn attitude you've ever conjured up. The second-guessing of God will finally come to an end, and a soul once desperately lost in its own despair will be filled with a newfound peace and a renewed hope, rejoicing *"in the Lord"* (Philippians 4:4, NASB) once again. The God, *"Who always leads us in triumph in Christ"* (2 Corinthians 2:14, AMP), is where the eyes of faith and a heart of trust must rest. It's the only way to go.

The hymn writer got it right.

> *Turn your eyes upon Jesus*
> *Look full in his wonderful face*

---

[87] Oswald Chambers (compiled and edited by Julie Ackerman Link), *Love: A Holy Command*, (Grand Rapids, Michigan, Discovery House, 2008), 29.

> *And the things of earth will grow strangely dim*
> *In the light of his glory and grace.*[88]

Second, surrender your dreams, agendas, plans, and purpose to God. The life motto of Charles Stanley was: "Obey God and leave all the consequences to him."[89] Good advice. We might consider following suit when approaching the trials and tribulations that come our way. Success in this world and victory in life depends on my willingness to *"discard everything…counting it all as garbage, so that I could gain Christ"* (Philippians 3:8, NLT).

Suffer the loss of everything—position, power, prestige, plans, possessions, etc.—for *"the infinite value of knowing Christ Jesus my Lord"* (Philippians 3:7, NLT). Nothing else really matters. C.S. Lewis penned the following:

> *Christ says, "Give me all. I don't want so much of your time and so much of your money and so much of your work: I want you. I have not come to torment your natural self. But to kill it. No half measures are any good. I don't want to cut off a branch here and a branch there, I want the whole tree down…I will give a new self instead. In fact, I will give you Myself: my own will shall become yours."*
>
> *The terrible thing, the almost impossible thing, is to hand over your whole self, all your wishes and precautions to Christ. But it is far easier than what we are trying to do instead…to remain what we call "ourselves," to keep personal happiness as our great aim in life.*[90]

---

[88] Helen Howarth Lemmel, Public Doman, 1922.
[89] Daniel Silliman, Died: Charles Stanley, In Touch preacher who led with stubborn faith. *Christianity Today*, April 18, 2023, retrieved from ttps://www.christianitytoday.com/news/2023/april/charles-stanley-died-in-touch-first-baptist-atlanta.html.
[90] Richard J. Foster and James Bryan Smith, editors, *Devotional Classics: Selected Readings for Individuals and Groups*, (New York, New York: Harper Collins, 1993), 8-9.

The remedy for being angry at God, when life turns messy and hard, rests in my surrender of what I value most, which is self. The first time John saw Jesus he knew that *"He must increase* (in all things and at all times), *but I must decrease"* (John 3:30). John the Baptist called for us all to relinquish control over the affairs of our daily lives. Stay out of God's business. He does not need your help. Trust the bigness, faithfulness, and love of the One Who rules over all things, *"visible and invisible,"* and who holds *"all things together"* (Colossians 1:16-18), including your life and mine. The plan and purpose of God for your life will eventually unfold in His time, His place, and in His way. Count on it.

Chad Scruggs, the senior pastor at Covenant Presbyterian Church, got the news that his nine-year-old daughter, Hallie Scruggs, was among three children and three adult staff members who were mercilessly gunned down and murdered at a Nashville Christian elementary school. A senseless act of violence and raw evil. A gunman entered the school and shot her victims dead. Hallie's father mournfully addressed the reporters. He appeared before reporters and spoke but a single sentence. He said, "Through tears we trust that she is in the arms of Jesus who will raise her to life once again."[91] That was it. Nothing more. Nothing more needed to be said, and he walked off to face a brutal reality.

Sadness in his voice? Yes. Grief? Yes, but not like those who have no hope (1 Thessalonians 4:13-14). Unimaginable pain? Yes. Anguish? Yes! Missing the laughter and joy, the hugs and kisses of that little girl? Yes. The emptiness of seeing a playroom now void of life? Yes! All of it! But he had no hint of rage and anger directed toward God. That may or may not come later in the dark places of his soul. But not then. Now, it was faith, a quiet resolve to rely on God and God alone and a simple, profound declaration of hope in

---

[91] Nick Reynolds, Pastor Shares 1-sentence response to daughter's death in Nashville shooting, *Newsweek*, March 28, 2023, retrieved from
https://www.newsweek.com/pastor-shares-1-sentence-response-daughters-death-nashville-shooting-1790900.

the Person and promises of God, despite the deepest of pain. The very presence of God was made evident in a few powerful words of courage and trust in *"the Father of mercies and the God of all comfort, who comforts us in all our affliction* (1 Corinthians 1:3-4, ESV).

In our brokenness, there may come a time to ask later, "Why? Why this? Why so young? Why her?" But for now, it is the time to look to Him, the only One able to heal a broken heart, to take solace in Him, to draw strength from Him to face another awful day—the very One who promised that *"if the Spirit of Him who raised Jesus from the dead lives in you* [and He does], *He who raised Christ Jesus from the dead will also give life to your mortal bodies* [and to that child] *through His Spirit, who lives in you* [and me, Halle, and the others]" (Romans 8:11, AMPC). And therein is hope, the realization that the best is yet to come. *"God will most certainly bring back to life those who died in Jesus"* (1 Thessalonians 4:13-14, MSG). It's never okay to be mad at God.[92] Leave your fury where it belongs, ultimately at the gates of hell.

"For Who has ever intimately known the mind of the Lord Yahweh well enough to become his counselor?" (1 Corinthians 2:16, ESV). A rhetorical question that demands a response. "No one!" Not you. Certainly not me.

In the introduction of her book, *Keep A Quiet Heart*, Elisabeth Elliot, wrote the following:

> *One rainy afternoon at Wheaton College in 1947 my friend Sarah Spiro and I were at the piano in Williston Hall. I had written down a few lines of a prayer which I hoped was poetry. Sarah studied them for a minute and then set them to music. I haven't a copy of the music, but here are the words:*

---

[92] Editors, Angry at God, *Billy Graham Evangelistic Association*, retrieved from https://peacewithgod.net/angry-at-god/?

*Lord, give to me a quiet heart
That does not ask to understand,
But confident steps forward in
The darkness guided by Thy hand.*

This was my heart's desire then. It is the same today. A willing acceptance of all that God assigns and a glad surrender of all that I am and have constitute the key to receiving the gift of a quiet heart. Whenever I have balked, the quietness goes. It is restored, and life immeasurably simplified, when I have trusted and obeyed.[93]

"Trust and obey for there is no other way to be happy in Jesus, but to trust and obey."[94] It's a good bet to willingly accept "all that God assigns to your life," because He loves you like nobody else can or will.

---

[93] Elizabeth Elliot, *Keep A Quiet Heart*, (Grand Rapids, Michigan: Revell), 12.
[94] John Henry Sammis (1846-1919), Lyrics, *Trust and Obey*, Public Domain, 1887.

> *Lord, why are you allowing this to happen to me? What have I done to deserve this? I've been faithful to you all these years and yet I'm suffering, and you just stand by and watch it happen. When are you going to call off the dogs.*
>
> –Bob Day, Retired Pastor and Friend

CHAPTER 6

When Are You Going to Call the Dogs Off?

One of the strongest persons I have ever met was my mother. She was one tough lady. She had to be. Life was hard from the time she was born into a family of seven children that survived the Great Depression of the 1920s to the day she died in her mid-eighties. I never once saw her curl up in a fetal position, put her thumb in her mouth, and cry like a baby in need. She was anything but weak of heart. Weakness was not in her DNA. As a single woman with little more than an eighth-grade education raising two kids, she set her "hands to the plow," and went to work to provide for the family. She lived by faith in God and the sweat of her brow. If anyone had the right to ask God, "When are you going to call the dogs off?", it would have been her.

One day, I asked her, "Mom, how did you do it? How did you survive all those years? How did you work, day after day, week after week with little to no rest, no help, and little encouragement to keep going and not quit? It would have been so easy for you to just walk out and walk away."

Her answer was revealing and challenging. She said, "You get up every morning, put both feet on the floor, place one foot in front of the other, and go do what you have to do."

I've never forgotten that. Paul Harvey said, "Someday I hope to enjoy enough of what the world calls success so that somebody will ask me, 'What's the secret of it?' I shall say simply this, 'I get up when I fall down.'"[95] Writer and artist, Mary Anne Radmacher, put it this way: "Courage doesn't always roar, sometimes it's the quiet voice at the end of the day whispering, 'I will try again tomorrow.'" That was my mother. I never once heard her ask God, "When will You call the dogs off?"

I can answer that: I don't know. Surprised? Frankly, my spiritual intellect is severely lacking. I cannot read God's mind (though I might like to), but even if I could, I wouldn't understand it anyway. His thoughts are rooted in infinite wisdom and locked away in eternity, and I'm not there yet. I do not, and never will this side of heaven, fully comprehend (if ever) God's blueprint, and neither am I able to figure out with any degree of consistency or logic what He has specifically and wondrously arranged and designed for me each day. I know only this. There is a divine plan second to none, and it's good, and I have a significant part to play in His story. I've also come to realize that nothing (no matter how painful it may be) will change in my life until He has accomplished and completed His good and perfect will. He cannot be, and will not be, deterred from His goals. *"But the LORD's plans stand firm forever; his intentions can never be shaken"* (Psalm 33:11).

Lisa TerKeurst suggested:

> *We have to fight the urge to expect our version of God's good timing, God's good provision, and God's good protection to match what we script for our lives. God Himself is good. And that means His plans are*

---

[95] Alice Gray, *More Stories for the Heart*, (Sisters, Oregon: Multnomah, 1997), 41.

good, His ways are good, and we can trust Him at all times.[96]

Maybe I should stop asking God to change His plans to accommodate my wishes, which often lack insight and clear direction. Oh, how I've struggled with that over the years. It's always better to remain confident in God (rather than self), knowing that He is at work in my life and yours. God's daily involvement and intervention (viewed sometimes as interference and invasion) is a sure thing. I can count on it. *"Many are the plans in a person's heart, but it is the Lord's purpose that prevails"*(Proverbs 19:21, NIV), and it is a good thing, too. With that, I am comforted and encouraged even in the most troubling of circumstances. God declared, *"I've said it, and I'll most certainly do it. I've planned it, so it's as good as done"* (Isaiah 46:10, MSG).

Theologian, Steve Lawson, a respected, seasoned, battle-tested pastor of many years and founder of OnePassion Ministries, said of God's authority and involvement in our daily, personal lives:

> *The Lord reigns,*
> *Not Satan, Not man.*
> *Not God AND man,*
> *Not 'good luck,'*
> *Not 'bad luck'*
> *Not random events,*
> *Not chance occurrences,*
> *Not the alignment of the stars,*
> *Not accidents,*
> *Not blind fate,*
> *Not good OR bad Karma;*
> *Only God and God alone!*[97]

God is fully aware of my plight and predicaments. He may very well have orchestrated the whole affair to bring about His

---

[96] Lisa TerKeurst, *FB Post*, May 3, 2023.
[97] John MacArthur and R.C. Sproul Fan Page, *FB Post*, September 2023.

purpose. Typically, I have asked God, "Why have you done this *to* me?" A better question might be, "Lord, why have you done this *for* me?" Perspective matters. He knows what's going on every day and why. *"It is good for me,"* wrote the psalmist, *"that I was afflicted, that I might learn your (God's) statutes"* (Psalm 119:71, KJV). God knows how badly I may be hurting. My heart is no surprise to Him.

The first time Moses met with God at the burning bush, the great I AM told him, *"I have surely seen the affliction of my people who are in Egypt,"* I heard *"their cry,"* and I'm *"aware* [know] *of their sufferings"* (Exodus 3:7), and that was over the span of some four centuries. *"I have seen," "I have given heed,"* and *"I have been aware"* are all perfect tense verbs, suggesting that the action of God in seeing, hearing, and knowing in the past was absolute, complete, and is carried forward to the present and on into the future. God is not hard of hearing, nor does He need or use Beltone hearing aids. He hears. He knows.

This was no informal relationship between God and Moses, nor was it some accidental meeting at a coffee house in Cairo, nor could it be considered celestial ease-dropping. Nothing could be further from the truth. Nothing about the lives of the Jews or my life for that matter has ever escaped God's notice. I have never been overlooked or forgotten in God's holy schemes, though I may have felt like it from time to time. In short, God is not ignorant of what was going on in the mud pits of Egypt nor is He unaware of the events taking place on the streets where you and I live. The psalmist wrote of God:

> **Psalm 139, 1-3, ESV** – *O Lord, you examine me and know me [That's intimidating].You know when I sit down and when I get up; even from far away you understand my motives [Uh-oh]. You carefully observe me when I travel or when I lie down to rest; You are aware of everything I do.*

That's scary as well as comforting. There is no hiding from the eyes of God that *"roam throughout the earth so that He may strongly support those whose heart is completely His* (2 Chronicles 16:9). But God also sees my foolishness. He sees it all even while I am in the "Valley of Ashes,"[98] a place in which we hide from God, "a place of gray desolation," spiritual poverty, "hopelessness and moral barrenness" found in the pursuit of pleasure as the highest ideal and the sole purpose of life.[99] Before God, the veneer is stripped away. I am totally exposed.

The fact of the matter is that God has always known me. He knows where I am, in despair or jubilation. He knows what I've been through, victory or defeat. He knows where I've been, in heaven or hell, and He knows where I'm going, running away or at peace. He knows just how much more trouble *I can take* before I break and fall apart. In fact, He knows what it *will take* to mold me and shape me into the man He wants me to be, taking everything He perfectly knows about me into account, and that includes my past blunders and successes, giftings and weaknesses, my present affairs and my future hopes and dreams. And yes, along the way toward His holy goal for my life, He may give you and me more pressure, more stress, more stretching, pulling and pushing than we really want or think we can bear at any given moment. *"Behold, like the clay in the potter's hand, so are you in My hand"* (Jeremiah 18:6), said the Lord. The work of the Potter is to accomplish His design for both my life and yours by any method He thinks necessary and best. *"I am certain,"* wrote Paul, *"that God, who began the good work within you, will continue his work until it is finally finished"* (Philippians 1:6, NLT). He knows where He is taking you and me,

---

[98] F. Scott Fitzgerald, *The Great Gatsby*, (Standard Ebooks, Public Doman), 28.
[99] Peter Conrad, Students/teacher comments about The Great Gatsby, *Welcome to Mr. Conrad's English 3 website*, retrieved from https://conradoehs.weebly.com/blog/the-great-gatsby-chapter-7-the-hottest-day-of-the-year#:~:text=The%20eyes%20of%20Dr.,behind%20Tom%2C%20Jordan%20and%20Nick.

and He knows how to get me there once the journey begins. He knows the valleys I am to walk. He knows the mountains I must scale. More to the point, God has a grand scheme, and He is fully committed to seeing it done no matter how long it may take or how hard it may prove to be. *"Nothing is impossible for God"* (Luke 1:37). Mary needed to be reminded of that when asked to bear the Son of God. So too did Abraham need such a reminder at an altar he built on Mt. Moriah to sacrifice his own son. *"Is anything too hard for the Lord?"* (Genesis 18:14). You need to answer that. So, do I.

The people of Israel were enslaved and subjected to the harsh, Egyptian taskmaster's whip, a perennial problem for four hundred years. They lived under severe conditions. Their very existence was marked by extremes. *"Bitter with hard labor"* (Exodus 1:14) was how Moses described it, an accurate summary of their daily lives. Their sons were murdered at birth (Exodus 1:16), a heartless act of unimaginable cruelty. Their futures were gone. Their hopes and dreams were crushed as they suffered year after year under the thumb of the Pharaohs, who were merciless and pulled the strings of every man, woman, and child under their authority. Slaves had few choices and no opportunities to alter their status or raise their social standing. Life was a dead-end street for most. Oppression, discouragement, fear, and despair were commonplace. Egypt ruled the day.

And prayers didn't seem to work, either. The people must have prayed (wouldn't you?), probably even begged God to help them. I certainly would have. But no immediate answer came from heaven. Tears were of no use. Whining and complaining bitterly to God had no tangible effect on their predicament. No hope in sight. No future. No way out. They doubtless wondered: when will the dogs be called off? When will things change? Will it ever get better? Will it ever end? It all sounds too familiar, if you ask me.

For Moses, the story begins with him boarding a "Carnaval cruise ship" (actually a wicker basket made of papyrus reeds) as a baby and then being cast adrift down the Nile for parts unknown. He was alone. No first-class accommodations here. No buffets. No lounge chairs on deck. No variety shows for entertainment. No casinos and one-armed slot machines or Black-Jack tables.

But he did find relief. For forty years, Moses was reared in the lap of luxury as the "adopted" son of Pharoah's daughter. That's all he knew in his younger days, until he fled Egypt as a murderer and ended up a sheepherder on the back side of the Midian Desert. God had him right where He wanted him....in the wilderness, God's schoolroom. There God worked him over, preparing His man to fulfill a role and task he never could have imagined. All went according to the divine plan, when God finally got his undivided attention in the desert at a *"bush...burning with fire"* (Exodus 3:2). Forty more years had passed by this time, and God was now ready to act redemptively and liberate His people. His plan unfolded like clockwork. The once prince of Egypt, a Jew, had been groomed for the last eighty years, and now was being formally commissioned by God to take the helm of leadership and bring Israel out of bondage. Eighty years of divine appointments and discouragements, difficulties, and trying experiences to prepare Moses to take on the might of Egypt and successfully lead the people out of slavery and into freedom for the first time in many a year. The "dogs" had bitten him, but Moses was now ready.

God's timetable is certain and unpredictable. His ways are undoubtedly above mine, frequently leaving me bewildered, desperate, shaken, and wondering if God will ever get around to ending my misery and relieving my pain. On more than one occasion, I've asked God to lighten up just a bit, especially when I'm tired of the battle and unable to make sense of the pain and suffering I'm experiencing. At times, I have fought to keep my head above water, get my emotions under control, clear my thinking, and attempt to decode God's next move, all to no avail. At times, my faith waned and wavered like riding the Screaming Eagle at

Dollywood. I wanted to believe that God has some grand scheme in view, but I needed some sense of clarification and reassurance. Sometimes that comes in retrospect by looking back over the events that have taken place in my life. Maybe the greatest battle of all, is learning to patiently wait on God to do something—anything—to help me out of a jam. The battle never seems to end. Courage and stamina are essential in life's journey for my survival and the success of God's mission accorded to me and you.

I remember Solomon's words:

> **Ecclesiastes 3:1-8, NIV** – *There is a time for everything, and a season for every activity under the heavens: a time to be born and a time to die…a time to mourn and a time to dance…a time to tear and a time to mend.*

Consequently, everything matters. Everything counts. Everything is important. Every day serves a particular function. Even the little things, good or bad, have an appointed time, a particular divine agenda, even at a *"burning bush"* in the desert or in a cave licking our wounds with the likes of Elijah. Following Alabama's recent loss to Texas as of this writing, head football coach Nick Saban revealed his approach to moving forward. He said, "You never want to waste a failing. Adversity can break some people and it can make some people great. It just depends on how you deal with it."

God never wastes a thing when it comes to my life. God got after Paul on the road to Damascus, the same man with a PhD in Old Testament Studies who hunted down, persecuted, stoned, and jailed first century Christians. God also likes going after reckless, prodigal sons who "squander" away their lives (Luke 15:11-32). Life is not haphazard or some accident waiting to happen. Stay the course until God changes it and/or changes you.

Proverbs 3:5-6, MSG – *Trust God from the bottom of your heart; don't try to figure out everything on your own. Listen for God's voice in everything you do, everywhere you go; He's the one who will keep you on track.*

Twice orphaned and stricken with crippling arthritis, Annie Johnson Flint, became a helpless invalid and eventually was institutionalized as her disease became worse with the passing of the years. "With a pen pushed through bent fingers and held by swollen joints,"[100] she wrote of her faith in the goodness and mercy of God, which never wavered in the forty years of continuous pain and limitations. She endured physical suffering throughout her life, yet managed to cling to God's inexhaustible grace through it all, and in the process, she helped thousands with her writings and poems of faith in the light of hardships and troubles.

Rowland V. Bingham, who wrote a short biography about Annie, remarked:

> *There were many times, no doubt, when her soul would be burdened with the mystery of it all and the why and wherefore of the thing that she was called to endure. In that respect she was most human like the rest of us, but the marvelous thing is that her faith never faltered, and that she was at all times able to say, "Thy will be done."*[101]

Annie Flint wrote the following short verse after meditating on 1 Corinthians 1:20, which says, *"For all the promises of God in him are yea, and in him, Amen."*

Is God? Does God?
Man's 'Why?' and 'How?'
In ceaseless iteration storm the sky.

---

[100] Rowland V. Bingham, Annie's Story, Bible Memory Association International, No copyright, no date, retrieved from http://www.homemakerscorner.com/ajf-annie.htm.
[101] Ibid.

> *'I am'; 'I will'; 'I do'—sure Word of God,*
> *Yea and Amen, Christ answers each cry;*
> *To all our anguished questionings and doubts*
> *Eternal affirmation and reply.*[102]

Annie was a realist and often wrote of life in a fallen world, but also spoke of the power of God's grace and the abundance of God's mercies to meet the needs of the day. Older saints will immediately recognize the following verse. We've sung it for years:

> *He giveth more grace as our burdens grow greater*
> *He sendeth more strength as our labors increase*
> *To added afflictions He addeth His mercy*
> *To multiplied trials He multiplies His peace*
>
> *When we have exhausted our store of endurance*
> *When our strength has failed ere the day is half done*
> *When we reach the end of our hoarded resources*
> *Our Father's full giving is only begun*
>
> *Fear not that thy need shall exceed His provision*
> *Our God ever yearns His resources to share*
> *Lean hard on the arm everlasting, availing*
> *The Father both thee and thy load will upbear*
>
> *His love has no limits, His grace has no measure*
> *His power no boundary known unto men*
> *For out of His infinite riches in Jesus*
> *He giveth, and giveth, and giveth again*[103]

The magnitude and intensity of Annie's trials and tribulations were never viewed by her as punishment or divine retribution for wrongful behavior or her failure to appease an angry God. Rather, they became useful instruments/tools in the hands of a Master Designer to bring good out of adversity and reshape a suffering woman whom God could use to touch the hearts of people

---

[102] Ibid.
[103] Annie Johnson Flint, "He Giveth More Grace," © Public Domain, retrieved from https://library.timelesstruths.org/music/He_Giveth_More_Grace/.

worldwide. She was born to carry the weight of ministry and privileged to share in *"the fellowship of His* [Christ's] *sufferings"* (Philippians 3:10).

The Apostle Paul spent three years in the deserts of Arabia (Galatians 1:17) and fourteen more years in Syria and Cilicia (Galatians 1:21). Every moment in the wilderness was profitable. There Paul learned the *"mysteries of God's will"* (Ephesians 1:9-11) and the stipulations of God's *"new covenant not of the letter, but of the Spirit"* (2Corinthians 3:6). The process of *"the renewing of* [his] *mind"* (Romans 12:2) started on a dusty road, all while he grew in his relationship to Christ as *"a bond-servant of God, and an apostle of Jesus"* (Titus 1:1). Once God completed His work, and not a second before, Paul emerged from the sands of the ancient world as the man who would write two-thirds of the New Testament. Every adversity, hardship, and difficulty were divinely employed to prepare God's man to serve God's Kingdom effectively. Nothing wasted. God's focus remained constant. Build the man. Prepare the man. Release the man to advance the Gospel and impact the generations to come.

In the face of uncertainty, Abraham was able to *"hope against hope"* (Romans 4:18), though the "dogs" were nipping at his heels for years. First, God put him in an untenable position where his faith would be tried and tested. God ordered him to pull up stakes and leave the comfort of his home and *"go forth from your country...to the land which I will show you"* (Genesis 12:1). The Epistle to the Hebrews states that *"he went out not knowing where he was going"* (Hebrews 11:8). Then there was a *"severe famine"* (Genesis 12:10) to deal with and subsequent trouble with the Egyptians (Genesis 12:12), a confrontation with Pharoah over Abram's wife, Sarai (12:18). And God still wasn't done. Tension and strife broke out within the family, causing a "church split" (Genesis 13:7). The devil loves that stuff. Lot went to *"the valley of the Jordan...as far as*

Sodom" and *"Abram settled in the land of Canaan"* (Genesis 13:11-12).

Then war came. Lot lost everything and Abram drew his sword and came to Lot's rescue. God then initiated the painful requirement for every male to be circumcised (Genesis 17:9-14) as a reminder that God means business and keeps His promises. His word and character are always at stake.

More trouble was coming. The fulfillment of God's promise to Abraham was delayed, and he and Sarah laughed at the prospect of having a child in their old age (Genesis 17:17). Sarah struggled with unbelief and pressed her Egyptian servant, Hagar, to have a baby with Abraham (Genesis 16:1). Abraham agreed with the plan. Of course, he did. Ishamel was born, and tension surfaced among all parties involved. However, God did what He said (He always does). Abraham was a hundred years old, and Sarah was ninety when she delivered Isaac. Abraham waited approximately twenty-five years for the birth of his promised son. In the interim, the couple learned that *"nothing is too difficult for the Lord"* (Genesis 18:14). *"Count the stars,"* God said to Abraham, *"So shall your descendants be"* (Genesis 15:5-6), and they are.

Again, God was not done. There was one final test. Abraham received direct orders from God to take Isaac to Mt. Moriah (Genesis 22), where he was to build an altar and prepare to sacrifice his son. He did as instructed and willingly laid his dreams aside as God commanded. A bold move. He trusted the *"God who gives life to the dead and calls into being that which does not exist"* (Romans 4:16). Abraham's belief held firm, though the "dogs" had been threatening through a series of troubling events, significant lapses in judgement, poor decisions, and struggles with trusting the word of God. That was Abraham's daily life: up and down, victories and defeats, and the testing and trials of his faith. God used it all to produce a man *"who would not waver in unbelief, but grew in faith"* (Romans 4:20). *"Against all odds, when it looked hopeless,*

Abraham believed the promise and expected God to fulfill it. He took God at his word, and as a result he became the father of many nations" (Romans 4:18, TPT). There was no hesitancy on the man's part to act in obedience. Just, *"Here I am."* No debilitating crisis of faith. No bargains with the Almighty. No pleading with God to "call the dogs off." A little faith can bring big results.

Standing on Mt. Moriah with a knife in his hand, Abraham confidently and quietly informed his son, *"God will provide for Himself the lamb for the burnt offering" (Genesis 22:8).* He trusted the promise and plan of God unreservedly, unwaveringly, and the pair confidently *"walked on together"* into their futures, knowing full well that the vision of becoming the *"father of many nations"* (Genesis 17:4-6, NIV) would come to fruition and God's word and plan would stand firm until all was completed and accomplished. Abraham counted on it. So can you.

> **Isaiah 55:11, AMP** – *So will My word be which goes out of My mouth; It will not return to Me void (useless, without result), Without accomplishing what I desire, And without succeeding in the matter for which I sent it.*

Throughout his life and ministry, Paul faced pain and suffering, *"afflicted in every way,"* trials and heartbreak, beatings and persecutions, sorrow and regret, (2 Corinthians 4:8-11), but he found relief and strength in the grace and mercy of God. He wrote:

> **2 Corinthians 4:16-18, MSG** – *So we're not giving up. How could we! Even though on the outside it often looks like things are falling apart on us, on the inside, where God is making new life, not a day goes by without his unfolding grace. These hard times are small potatoes compared to the coming good times, the lavish celebration prepared for us. There's far more here than meets the eye. The things we see now*

> *are here today, gone tomorrow. But the things we can't see now will last forever.*

And that is where we must focus our eyes, not on this transient realm, but on the results found only in eternity, in a life beyond this crazy world.

In her devotional, *Edges of His Way*, Amy Carmichael explains:

> *The trial of our faith* [whatever it may be] *works more and more, while we look not at it, but away from it to that which lies beyond....the things which are seen try to distract us from the things that are not seen (the eternal weight of glory – 2 Corinthians 4:17-18, KJV).*[104]

> *Great Son of Man, who walked our dust,*
> *Thy love will not forget...*
> *And let the things which are not seen*
> *Shine like stars at night*
> *Till all the space that lies between*
> *Be filled with (Thy) light.*[105]

When called by God to do the unthinkable, Abraham responded with a simple, *"Here I am"* Genesis 22:11). Just that. No more. No less. One short Hebrew word, *hin·nê·nî*. Short, sweet, and to the point. In the midst of his greatest trial, he declared his readiness to accept God's judgements whatever they may be for himself and for his son. We can do no less in the thick of our own struggles. No rebellious anger. No excessive worry or doubts. No second-guessing. No crippling fear, heavy depression, or despondency over what God had asked him to do: place his precious son on the altar of sacrifice and potentially destroy their futures and

---

[104] Amy Carmichael, *Edges of His Ways*, (Fort Washington, Pennsylvania: CLC Publications, 1955), 166.
[105] *Ibid*, 167.

dreams. The thrust of a knife could not ever kill the divine plan, and Abraham believed it. He knew it. He lived it.

Robert Rogers (1731-1795), a British soldier and an American colonial frontiersman said, "My faith didn't remove the pain, but it got me through the (agony and aching of my heart). Trusting God didn't diminish or vanquish the anguish, but it enabled me to endure it."[106]

In her book, *Holding on to Hope*. Nancy Guthrie shared her experience with the death of her daughter:

> *We had Hope (her infant daughter) for 199 days (about 6 months). We loved her. We enjoyed her richly and shared her with everyone we could. We held her during seizures. Then we let her go.*
>
> *The day after we buried Hope, my husband said to me, "You know, I think we expected our faith to make this hurt less, but it doesn't." ...Our faith keeps us from being swallowed by despair. But I don't think it makes our loss hurt any less.*
>
> *Early on in my journey, I said to God, "Okay, if I have to go through this, then give me everything. Teach me everything you want to teach me through this. Don't let this incredible pain be wasted in my life!"*
>
> *God allows good and bad into our lives, and we can trust him with both. ...Trusting God when the miracle does not come, when the urgent prayer gets no answer, when there is only darkness, this is the kind of faith God values most of all.*
>
> *I believe that the purpose of Hope's short life, and my life, was and is to glorify God.*[107]

---

[106] Nancy Perpall, *Around Which All Things Bend*, (Bloomington, Indiana: Archway Publishing, 2022), 60.
[107] Nancy Guthrie, *Holding on to Hope*, (Wheaton, Illinois: Tyndale, 2015) 9, 44.

No need to call the dogs off. They serve the greater plans of God for your life and mine.

Do you doubt the love of God? Why? Because of the bad things that He allows to happen to good people? Because of the unfairness and injustice and suffering and pain and cruelty of life? Some questions we won't have answers for, until we get to heaven. But one thing we can know for sure is that God loves you and me. How do we know that? We know just by looking at the cross where He proved His love for the world that mocks Him, ignores Him, despises Him, scorns Him, and rejects Him. May .... we look at the cross and see "I love you," written in red .... the red of the Saviour's blood. Surely we can say with the hymn writer, "Oh how He loves you and me."[108]

–Denis Lyle, Irish pastor

CHAPTER 7

What Have I Done to Deserve This?

One day, my seven-year-old daughter stopped me and asked, "Daddy, does God really love us like you say He does?" I said, "Yes! Of course He does. He loved you before you were born. He still loves you today, and He will always love you, come what may." Thinking I was done with our conversation, I turned to go on my way.

But she followed with one final question. "Well, how can He love us after all the things we have done?"

From the mouths of babes, the innocence of a little girl with pigtails wondering if God would continue to love her, even if she did something terribly wrong. She wasn't looking for an excuse to misbehave or avoid accountability. She was looking for clarification. Could she (and the rest of us) expect mercy from God when we screw up? Is there mercy for a rebel like me, like you, *"doing what (we) feel like doing, when (we) feel like doing it"*

---

[108] Denis Lyle, The love of God, *Pastor Life*, retrieved from
http://sermons.pastorlife.com/members/sermon.asp?SERMON_ID=4194&fm=author bio&authorid=3360.

(Ephesians 2:4-5, MSG)? The answer lies in the heart of God, *"who is rich in mercy, because of the great love he has for us, gave us life...God's gift to you"* (Ephesians 2:4-5, PHILLIPS).

Actually, I've done plenty to deserve *"the wrath of God...like everyone else"* (Ephesians 2:3, PHILLIPS), because of my personal *"trespasses and sins"* (Ephesians 2:1). I didn't get what I deserve. Instead, I was given God's love and mercy freely, and as the song title states, *I Will Sing of the Goodness of God.*[109] *"I will sing of the mercy and loving-kindness of the Lord forever; (and) make known Your (God's) faithfulness from generation to generation"* (Psalm 89:1, AMPC).

The answer to my daughter's question is straightforward and clear. *"The steadfast love of the LORD is from everlasting to everlasting" (Psalm 103:17).* That means forever, without end, without change, without bias, without conditions. He loves because He wants to. End of story. It is His nature. *"God is love"* (1 John 4:8, 16). And so, *"we have confidence for the day of judgment...There is no fear in love, but perfect love casts out fear. For fear has to do with punishment"* (1 John 4:17-18, ESV). The cross put an end to that once and for all. The question is settled forever. The wrath of God was poured out at Calvary where Christ became *"the propitiation for our sins...and not for ours only but also for the sins of the whole world"* (1 John 2:2). In other words, God is not mad at me anymore and neither is He mad at a little seven-year-old girl. He never will be.

John the Baptist's entire life and ministry was devoted to and influenced by one specific truth. His father, Zacharias, said it: *"The heart of our God is full of mercy toward us,* (Luke 1:78, PHILLIPS). Every action of God is driven by an indescribable, remarkable love, a love so deep and rare you can only find it on the outskirts of eternity and only when God chooses to send it our way. He shed His

---

[109] Jenn Johnson, *I Sing of the Goodness of God*, Bethel Music, 2019.

love for us in the person of Jesus, His only Son, and into the lives of countless needy people down through the ages. Spurgeon said, "God made heaven and earth with his fingers, but he gave his Son with his heart in order that he might save sinners."[110] That's you and me. There is no greater love than that (John 15:13).

You may feel otherwise when walking through hell, when life gets you down, when things are not going well, when setbacks keep coming, and when problems keep mounting. The meds are not working, and the pantry is empty, the money is running out, and you've lost your job and maybe your health. Your car has been repossessed. Your home is in foreclosure. Your dignity and self-worth is shot to pieces. When nothing is left, and you've come to the end of yourself, there you will find God, or you may be tempted to think your pain and suffering is the result of something you've done to warrant God's disfavor and anger. That is not the case.

> *You are not too dirty for God to cleanse.*
> *You are not too broken for God to fix.*
> *You are not too far for God to reach.*
> *You are not too guilty for God to forgive.*
> *And you are not too worthless for God to love.*
>
> –Anonymous

A good word for people who are troubled about the greatest love and mercy the world has ever known.

The Humaita Prison in São José dos Campos, Brazil, was founded in 1972 by a group of Catholics from the local diocese. An association was formed between the Fraternity of Assistance to the Convicted (APAC) and Prison Fellowship International in the United States. The focus was to address the deplorable conditions in Brazil's other detention centers. The Humaita Prison became a

---

[110] Charles Hadden Spurgeon, The tender mercies of God, *The Spurgeon Center for Biblical Preaching at Midwestern* Seminary, June 27, 1886, retrieved from https://www.spurgeon.org/resource-library/sermons/the-tender-mercy-of-god/#flipbook/.

model of reform, run on the principles of God's love and the respect and dignity every person, prisoner or otherwise, deserves. It was a prison like no other. No armed guards. No high-tech security systems, and some prisoners were released daily to work jobs outside the walls of incarceration. The founders called it "restorative justice," and it's working. The recidivism rate among the prisoners is a mere four percent. One inmate who escaped from six other prisons was asked why he did not attempt to escape anymore. "*Do amor ninguém foge,*" he replied, "Nobody flees from love."[111]

Chuck Colson visited the prison and saw firsthand the new system at work. The answer to its success soon became apparent. An inmate guide escorted Colson to a room that was used for solitary confinement and punishment. The cell always housed the same convict. At the end of a long concrete corridor, the prison guide put his key into the lock, turned back to look at Colson, and asked, "Are you sure you want to go in?"

"Of course, I've been in isolation cells all over the world."

Slowly, the massive doors swung open, and Colson saw the prisoner in that cell: "a (lone) crucifix, beautifully carved Jesus, hanging on the cross." The guide said softly, "He's doing time for the rest of us."[112]

That's mercy, God reaching into a prison cell. It's the cross where bruised and bloodied humanity comes to embrace the offer of the love and forgiveness of God in Christ Jesus. It is the very place where droplets of life-giving, cleansing blood flow down from "*an old rugged cross*" and falls lovingly and mercifully upon the souls of broken people. That's the Gospel, "*the power of God for salvation to everyone who believes, to the Jew first and also to the Greek*" (Romans 1:16-18). The Gospel is mercy for all men and women

---

[111] Stephen G. Adubato, 'Nobody flees from love': Brazil's alternative prisons offer a model of restorative justice," *Jesuit Review*, November 17, 2021, retrieved from https://www.americamagazine.org/politics-society/2021/11/17/brazil-alternative-prison-restoration-apac-241703.

[112] Chuck Colson, Humaita Prison, *Guidepost*, January 1995.

everywhere—for the prisoner needing to be set free from moral failures to experience the best God has to offer in this life and the life to come, for the spiritually blind who must see the truth and the reality of God and find the only way to life eternal, for the lame who stumble through broken relationships needing strength to rise up and *"walk in love (*Ephesians 5:2), for the foolish man who needs *"wisdom from above"* (James 1:13) to successfully blaze a new path toward abundant living (John 10:10), and for the wounded and despondent heart who needs healing and wholeness. It's mercy from start to finish, for all men and women no matter their status or station in life, the color of their skin, or the national allegiance or background. How can God love me after the things I've done? The answer is profound. It's simply His good pleasure to do so. That's it. I kneel like all men must, solely dependent upon the good graces and mercy of God, which He gives freely and generously.

Saul had "shamefully treated and laid waste the church continuously [with cruelty and violence]; and entering house after house, he dragged out men and women and committed them to prison" (Acts 8:3, AMPC). He approached the high priest at Damascus to issue credentials authorizing him to hunt down members of "the Way" (Acts 9:2), arrest them, chain them, and drag them back to Jerusalem for prosecution. In today's world, Saul might be considered a middle eastern terrorist, an extremist, similar in practice and zeal to a card-carrying member of the Taliban. He wanted nothing less than ridding Israel of Christian influence. Saul would stop at nothing. He was in on the stoning of Stephen, as well (Acts 7:58-8:1). Saul was one angry, hateful man, "a Hebrew of Hebrews...a Pharisee" (Philippians 3:5), an extraordinary candidate for God's extraordinary love, grace, and mercy. God caught up with him on a dusty road and dramatically changed his life forever. Once a man of unyielding law and merciless judgement, now a man full of grace and truth in Christ Jesus. Once a disgruntled and troubled man, now a man set free and clean by the cross of Christ. "Do not call something unclean if God has made it clean" (Acts 10:15, 28, NLT).

Paul was forgiven. His past was gone. His slate was clean. He was made a new man by the love of God. Given a new focus. Found a new priority. Inherited a new life. What nobody else could see in Paul (and in you and me), God saw, despite that the man's hands were stained with the blood of the saints. God sees in me more than I see in myself, more than my sin will permit me to see about my value and worth in this world. God sees me differently. I see myself as a rebellious, foolish prodigal. God sees me as the son who made poor decisions and got himself into trouble and needs help. I had gone astray, but *"when (I) came to (my) senses, "* (Luke 15:17, NIV), I came home to my Father's house and was welcomed with joy, and a party to celebrate my return. God sees my potential. He sees my promise. He sets His sights beyond my failures and weakness, seeing not what I was, nor what I am, but what I could be to the glory of God.

In 1917, life had gotten hard for Frederick M. Lehman, a German born man who was converted to Christianity at age eleven. Eventually, he entered the pastoral ministry, serving churches in Iowa, Indiana, and Missouri. However, his personal finances soon dried up. The churches could no longer support him. Little money was available to "make ends meet" and feed his family of eight children, and still continue in his ministry. He "found himself working in a lemon and orange packing factory in Pasadena, moving thirty tons of produce daily." One day, during his work break, he sat on an empty crate and began thinking hard about the wonder of God's love, given the stress and pressure in his life. Amid his despair and perplexity, with little going for him, he picked up pen and paper and wrote these magnificent words:

> *The love of God is greater far, than tongue or pen can ever tell. It goes beyond the highest star and reaches to the lowest hell...God gave his Son to win. His*

erring child he reconciled and pardoned from his sin."[113]

It is the very heart of God, the story of His great love and abundant mercy.

The "good news" is that God entered my misery, my pain and suffering, my disappointments, my doubts and fears and then poured His life into my soul, giving me love, joy, peace of mind and heart, patience/forbearance, faith, hope, kindness, goodness, gentleness, and self-control (Galatians 5:22-23, NIV). It is what the love of God does best.

As a child of God, adopted (Romans 8:15) into His family as His son and/or daughter, there is nothing you can do to disqualify yourself from God's love and His favor. He is *"Abba Father,"* Who:

> **Ephesians 1:4-6, MSG** – *Long before he laid down earth's foundations, he had us in mind, had settled on us as the focus of his love, to be made whole and holy by his love. Long, long ago he decided to adopt us into his family through Jesus Christ.* [What pleasure he took in planning this!] *He wanted us to enter into the celebration of his lavish gift-giving by hand of his beloved Son.*

God is in the business of purposely enlarging His family,[114] and He has had you and me *"in mind...as the focus of his love"* from the beginning.

Let me say it again: God is not mad at you. You are not trash to be discarded. He has not written you off. He has not wiped His hands clean of you. If you stumble and fall along life's rocky path with all its twists and turns, He is there, ready to pick you up, dust you off, and get you moving again. *"But You, LORD, are a shield*

---

[113]Robert J. Morgan, *Then Sings My Soul*, (Nashville, Tennessee: Thomas Nelson, 2003), 276-277.

[114] Ligonier Teaching Fellows, Adoption into God's family, *Ligonier Ministry*, Oct 2, 2010, retrieved from https://www.ligonier.org/learn/devotionals/adoption-into-gods-family#:~:text=We%20have%20been%20brought%20into,8%3A15).

around me, My glory, and the One who lifts my head" (Psalm 3:3). His love and mercy are without parallel.

In 1912, James Rowe and Howard E. Smith, wrote a hymn to reassure and remind people of the love and mercy of God. It is a great hymn sung by churches for more than a hundred years, called "Love Lifted Me." It is based on the story of the disciples caught in a storm with driving winds and pounding waves threatening their very lives (Matthew 14:22-33). They were afraid of going under and drowning in the rough seas. Then they saw Jesus walking on water toward them.

> *I was sinking deep in sin*
> *Far from the peaceful shore*
> *Very deeply stained within*
> *Sinking to rise no more*
> *But the master of the sea*
>
> *Heard my despairing cry,*
> *From the waters lifted me*
> *Now safe am I*
>
> *Love lifted me!...*
> *When nothing else could help*
> *Love lifted me.*

The words of that splendid hymn forms the very essence of the Gospel story and message. Amidst the storms and fears that often accompany daily living, God shows up. He comes to rescue, to encourage, to calm the hearts of men and women struggling to keep their heads above water. He comes because He loves us, warts and all. He loves you in your weakness, in your brokenness, hopelessness, doubts, unbelief, and in your failures. *"Love knows no limit to its endurance, no end to its trust, no fading of its hope; it can outlast anything. It is, in fact, the one thing that still stands when all else has fallen* (1 Corinthians 13:7-8, PHILLIPS).

David, the adulterer and murderer, begged God, " Have mercy on me, O God, according to your unfailing love; according to your great compassion blot out my transgressions" (Psalm 51:1, NIV). And there it is. "Unfailing love" and "great compassion" form the foundation upon which mercy happens. Mercy is action. Mercy is leniency. Mercy is forgiving the offender. Mercy does not demand retribution.

A former member of a white-supremacy group, who was sentenced to thirty years in prison for attempting to plant a bomb at the home of a Jewish businessman, nearly lost his life trying to escape the police. He was shot. It was a miracle he did not die. He later said, "He [God] didn't give me what I deserved. But because he is full of grace and mercy, he gave me exactly what I needed." God changed his life. God did not bring the hammer of justice down. The Judge of the universe made a final decision. He would transform the man's heart and his future, and make him a campus minister, the pastor of a local church, and a teacher and writer at the C.S. Lewis Institute.[115]

That's mercy, a compassionate and loving hand extended by God to those buried in the rubble of their own moral failures. Sometimes He withholds the consequences of poor behavior. Sometimes He does not. There is but one significant reason, one divine goal for making that holy decision: the long term, permanent, healing of the soul. God is not interested in temporary relief or easy fixes. No. Whatever is best and necessary for fully redeeming a life over the long haul, He uses it all to accomplish a wholeness that will last a lifetime in this world and on into eternity. Mercy uses even the stupidity of our decisions and the pain and suffering associated with sin as divine, Holy Spirit therapy to challenge and alter my life for the better. Mercy always trumps judgement, because it is grounded in the love of God, and His faithfulness – the God Who promises to

---

[115] Thomas Tarrants, "God's Mercy to a Klansman," *CT magazine* (September, 2020), 79-80

forgive the past and refuses to remember the wrong committed. Charles Finney (the Father of American revivalism) described his conversion to Christianity at twenty-nine years old like this:

> *The Holy Spirit ... seemed to go through me, body and soul." He later wrote. "I could feel the impression, like a wave of electricity, going through and through me. Indeed it seemed to come in waves of liquid love, for I could not express it in any other way.*

And neither can I, not with "waves of liquid love," washing away my sin, pressing me to leave yesterday behind, start afresh, and look toward a new future with high expectations. *"He saved us, not because of the righteous things we had done, but because of his mercy. He washed away our sins, giving us a new birth and new life through the Holy Spirit"* (Titus 3:5, NLT). It's mercy freely given by God, washing over my soul, cleaning up my act, and releasing me from the prison and filth of my own guilt and shame, to live better than I have ever before. Divine love causes God to let go of my past, hold back His wrath, and sometimes shields me from the consequences I'm justly due for my wrongdoing. *"God being rich in mercy, because of His great love with which He loved us...made us alive together with Christ"* (Ephesians 2:4-5).

Jeremiah stood looking over the condition of the city of Jerusalem. What he saw was defeat, desolation, destruction, famine, starvation, and affliction. It sounds like a running commentary on many a life. *"Mourning and moaning"* was the order of the day. Israel had been *"swallowed up"* (2:5) in their misery, because *"Jerusalem (had) sinned greatly"* (Lamentations 1:8). They rebelled and shed tears over the judgement of God that had come upon them by means of the Babylonians (586 BC). The city was overrun, and Israel had been carried away into captivity. *"My eyes,"* Jeremiah cried, *"run down with water"* (Lamentations 1:16). The city had collapsed. Nothing was left. At his lowest point, spiritually and mentally discouraged, the prophet remembered the Lord (good moved when depressed and despondent). *"This I recall to my mind,"* he wrote:

> **Lamentations 3:22-23** – *The faithful love of the LORD never ends. His mercies never cease. Great is his faithfulness; His mercies begin afresh each morning.*

I've got to straighten out my thinking…clear my eyes and see life from a different perspective, through the eyes of faith and the truth of God's Word. God is faithful and merciful every day, from the rising and setting of the sun to the nightly appearance of the moon and stars.

On November 13, 2004, a few weeks before Thanksgiving, Victoria Ruvolo was driving home from watching her niece sing at a recital on Long Island, when an eighteen year old boy, Ryan Cushing, threw a frozen, twenty pound turkey through her windshield. The turkey was purchased with a stolen credit card. She survived, but Mrs. Ruvolo sustained serious injuries, including brain trauma. Her face was shattered. The bones in her cheek and jaw were crushed. The socket of her left eye was fractured, and her esophagus caved in. She required extensive reconstructive surgery and nine months of rehabilitation.

Prosecutors pushed for a maximum sentence of twenty-five years in prison for first-degree assault. To everyone's surprise, Mrs. Ruvolo argued before the judge and the court for the young man to be shown mercy, compassion, and kindness. She pressed for a lighter sentence. She said, "I didn't want Ryan to rot in jail." Nearly a year later, Mr. Cushing pled guilty to all charges. Afterwards, he stopped to speak to Victoria in the courtroom and wept. She embraced him.

Sobbing, he said, "I'm so sorry. I didn't mean it."

"It's okay," she replied. "I just want you to make your life the best it can be."

Some months later, following his sentencing, Ryan told his victim, "Your ability to forgive has had a profound effect on me. It has already made a positive change in my life."

Quietly, she responded, "There is no room for vengeance in my life. I know you are remorseful."

Mr. Cushing was sentenced to six months in prison and five years' probation. Mercy, mercy, mercy! It made a difference. He went on to be a productive member of society. Somebody said of Victoria, "That's her legacy. She's an example of forgiveness in a vengeful world."[116]

God is not out to get you or me. His "legacy" is mercy. He is not, as some think, desiring to prosecute me to the full extent of the law, His law. He loves to forgive, restore, and release people. A friend of mine, who has lived many years in spiritual and physical adversity, suggested that many people, including Christians, view their suffering in this world as a result of God's punishment "for some secret sin they have committed against His Holiness." A great insight, but a tragic approach to life.

> *The fact is," he went on to say, "our suffering may be for the benefit of someone else and has nothing to do with God's judgment on our life... I'm under the impression that some of us were saved so that we might die well in the presence of an unbelieving world.*[117]

God is not the prosecuting attorney, and He should not be perceived, as such. He took care of my guilt that "Good Friday" when Jesus stood in my place before all heaven and the demons of hell, bearing my shame and guilt (and I have plenty of that) in the courtroom of Calvary where the Son of God was tried, convicted,

---

[116] Richard Sandomir, Victoria Ruvolo, Who Forgave Her Attacker, Is Dead at 59, *The New York Times*, March 28, 2019, Retrieved from
https://www.nytimes.com/2019/03/28/obituaries/victoria-ruvolo-dead.html
[117] A thought shared with me by my friend Bob Day.

and sentenced to die for yours and my transgressions. It is why the mercy of God can be extended and applied to my life, the very cause behind God loving me no matter what, even after the things I have done. My rap sheet is longer than I care to admit.

Betsie ten Boom, fell ill and died on December 16, 1944, under deplorable conditions at Ravensbrück (a Nazi concentration camp). She used to say to Corrie her sister, "There is no pit so deep that God's love is not deeper still."[118] How right she was.

When we open the Bible, we encounter a very different God. He is our *"Advocate"* (1 John 2:1) who takes up our cause. He has never lost a case.

The devil has dragged me before the tribunal of God. He has irrefutable facts about my life. They are painfully revealed and accurate: *"evil dwells in me...making me a prisoner"* (Romans 7:21, 23). The Judge is not surprised by any of it. Nothing is hidden, "dirty laundry and all." My Attorney stands to make His case. The truth is presented to the heavenly court: *the "Lamb of God"* has taken away my sin and my guilt (John 1:29). On my behalf, a *"great cloud of witnesses"* are called to the stand to testify. The defense rests its case, and the jurors are sent out to consider the evidence against me. They return shortly with the final verdict. All present in the courtroom of heaven rise to hear the decision that will decide my fate for all eternity. The great Judge of the universe quiets the courtroom and speaks with authority. He reads the findings of the jurors with a smile. "Innocent on all counts. All charges are dismissed." *"There is, therefore, now no condemnation for those who are in Christ Jesus"* (Romans 8:1). The courtroom of angels and saints of every age erupts with shouts of joy and thanksgiving. *"Salvation to our God who sits on the throne, and to the Lamb"* (Revelation 7:10). A final word is spoken from the throne of grace

---

[118] Kaylena Radcliff, A war story: 'There is no pit so deep God's love is not deeper still,' *Christian History Institute, Issue #121,* 2017, retrieved from https://christianhistoryinstitute.org/magazine/article/there-is-no-pit-so-deep.

and mercy, *"Set (him) free"* (Romans 7:24). Justice is served. *"You shall know the truth, and the truth shall set you free"* (John 8:32).

This is the God who delights in you, the God who sings over you, the God who rescues and redeems. "The Lord your God is with you, the Mighty Warrior who saves. He will take great delight in you; in his love he will no longer rebuke you but will rejoice over you with singing" (Zephaniah 3:17).

That's God's legacy: love and mercy in a "vengeful world." That's the God who loves you and me "after all the things we have done," and will continue to do so, *"from everlasting to everlasting."*

> *Out of suffering have emerged the strongest souls; the most massive characters are seared with scars.*
>
> — Kahlil Gibran, writer, poet, and artist

CONCLUSION

The Healing Balm

In 1966, a Welsh mining tragedy in the town of Aberfan claimed the lives of a hundred and sixteen children between the ages of seven to eleven years old. All of them were students at Pantglass Junior School. The lives of twenty-eight adults ended that day, as well. An avalanche of black coal waste buried the school and several houses located near the base of a mountain of coal sledge.[119] A thirty-foot tall "tsunami of sludge" broke loose and raced "down the hill at a speed of more than eighty miles per hour.

On the 27th of October, a mass burial of eighty-one children took place in the town's cemetery. Twelve thousand mourners stood with their heads bowed low at the funeral, devastated by their great loss. A simple thirteen-minute ceremony was held while all over Britain flags flew at half-mast and memorial services were conducted at churches and chapels throughout Wales.[120] The entire country grieved. The depth of pain that day and in the days to come

---

[119] 'UK: Mass Funeral Of 81 Children At Aberfan 1966,' Video, British Pathe, Reuters, Nov 10, 1966, retrieved from
https://britishpathe.com/video/VLVA6RW5Q4G3MPQZNKD2KBXYQ6FN6-RTV.

[120] Meilan Solly, Associate Editor, History, The true story of the Aberfan disaster, *Smithsonian Magazine,* November 15, 2019, retrieved from
https://www.smithsonianmag.com/history/true-story-aberfan-disaster-featured-crown-180973565/

for each family was indescribable. During those heartbreaking moments, God was there in the thick of the gathered crowds to collect their tears in His bottle, keep track of all their sorrows, and log each hurt and loss in His book (Psalm 56:8, NLT). So wrote David when he was in trouble and life seemed out of control.

The mourners prayed and read Scripture. *"Allow the children to come to Me; do not forbid them, for the kingdom of God belongs to such as these"* (Mark 10:14). Sadness, a deep emptiness, and anger were directed at the negligence of government officials, who had refused to act even after being repeatedly warned of the potential problem. Their disregard and callousness turned deadly and robbed a small town of its children.

The villagers would never see their children again this side of a distant eternity. They stood looking over the mass grave, surely trying to make sense of the whole ordeal. But there were no immediate answers. No acceptable clarification of purpose or meaning. No opinions worth hearing. No excuses worthy of consideration. No Christian platitudes that could cover the hurt and loss. They simply experienced bewilderment, overwhelming grief, and the deepest of remorse.

Nevertheless, at the close of the service, the crowd sang, "Jesus, Lover of My Soul," written by Charles Wesley in 1790. Collectively, they turned to the only One who could help them pick up the pieces, find some peace and comfort, restore some level of sanity and normalcy to their daily lives, heal their broken hearts, and calm the tempest of uncertainty, anger, doubts, and fears. Below the feet of the crowd was a row of coffins that could not be ignored or wished away. The graves of some eighty children lay before the mourners. There was no escaping reality. Tragedy had struck and taken its toll.

Those present did what some might consider courageous, unthinkable, and certainly unexpected. They bowed their heads in reverence to God and began to sing quietly the words of that great hymn as they dared to stare down death.

> *Jesus, lover of my soul,*
> *Let me to Thy bosom fly,*
> *While the nearer waters roll,*
> *While the tempest still is high.*
> *Hide me, O my Savior, hide,*
> *Till the storm of life is past...*
> *Other refuge have I none,*
> *Hangs my helpless soul on Thee;*
> *Leave, ah! Leave me not alone,*
> *Still support and comfort me.*
> *All my trust on Thee is stayed,*
> *All my help from Thee I bring;*
> *Cover my defenseless head*
> *With the shadow of Thy wing.*[121]

So often in times like these, questions arise, targeted at God to account for His whereabouts and His actions—or seemingly lack thereof. Where was God in all this? Couldn't He have stopped it? Lord, why? Why did this have to happen? Why didn't You step in before the tragedy? What purpose did all this serve?

All those young lives, gone. I want answers when life goes south, and the days turn dark and uncertain. I need "support and comfort" and reassurance amidst the gloom. I need a place to rest my trust in the sovereignty of God when life remains a mystery and there seems to be no explanation or justification for what has happened.

Like many of you, I've found it difficult to cling to the goodness and wisdom of God—that He knows what He's doing. I've needed Heaven to dry my eyes and pour into my heart the "healing balm" of God's love. I need the God of Isaiah Who has

---

[121] Charles Wesley, *Jesus, Lover of My Soul*, Public Domain, 1740, retrieved from https://library.timelesstruths.org/music/Jesus_Lover_of_My_Soul/

"called you (and me) by name," Who is for me and with me, especially when I'm drowning in sadness and hopelessness (Isaiah 43:1-3) and when there seems to be no accounting for the tragic events of the day. The hymn writers were correct:

> *I need Thee (God) every hour,*
> *In joy or pain;*
> *Come quickly and abide,*
> *Or life is vain.*[122]

I am overwhelmed and dwarfed by the courage and faith of those at Aberfan who could sing of God's faithfulness. In their grief, they found the only One able to heal the wounds of a soul in sorrow. He alone would give much needed comfort, genuine support, and hope for today, and most importantly, hope for tomorrow. It is life lived under the shadow of God's wing. Robert Morgan, who authored *The Strength You Need*, wrote:

> *There comes a time when all we can do is live by faith (and sometimes my faith is not to strong). We can't figure things out; we can't explain things; we can't solve or disentangle them; we can't clarify them or clear them up. We have no answers; we only have the Lord.*[123]

That's enough. In the toughest of times, when life is messy and hard, you will discover that God's *"grace is sufficient"* (2 Corinthians 12:9) for the day and for the days to come.

In my weakness and arrogance, I continue to bombard God with questions, demanding answers, asking God to explain Himself, as if I had the right or the slightest chance of understanding the deepest of truths and the secrets of the triune God.

Evelyn Underhill (1875-1941), who wrote extensively on the spiritual life for ordinary people, put all my troubling days and

---

[122] Robert Lowery and Annie S. Hawks, *I Need Thee Every Hour*, Public Doman, 1883.
[123] Robert J. Morgan, *The Strength You Need*, (Nashville, Tennessee: W Publishing, 2016) 123.

demanding questions directed toward heaven in proper perspective. She said, *"This is the secret of joy. We shall no longer strive for our own way; but commit ourselves, easily and simply, to God's way, acquiesce in His will, and in so doing find our peace."*[124]

So much for my questions. They seem rather petty at times and certainly prideful in light of the authority and power of God. Better I put an end to my complaining and shouting at Him. Neither does any good. Rather, it's best to open my heart, and fully *"yield myself"* to Him in order to *"accomplish"* His Word and will in every circumstance and aspect of my life, whether I like it or not. God knows what He wants, and He knows how, when, and where He wants to accomplish His goals (not mine or yours). I may find that as my questions decrease in frequency and intensity, my submission to Him rises, and joy and contentment returns to my soul.

Clemson head football coach Dabo Swinney was asked by a journalist, "When you hoist a trophy, you spend time talking about God and faith and what's above everything else, not just football. Can you speak about that a little bit more?" He responded:

> *Well, I mean, to me, that's just the priorities of my life… it's hard to survive and thrive in this world if you don't have a spiritual foundation…because life is hard, and we're all going to experience death and failure and setbacks and disappointments and (maybe) cancer and — it's just a really difficult world. For me, my relationship with Christ has given me hope and peace.*

Dabo then quoted Jeremiah 29:11. "'For I know the plans I have for you,' declares the Lord, 'plans to prosper you and not to harm you, plans to give you hope and a future.'" He said:

> *I've always taken that, and I've kind of applied that to my life along my journey. If there's really hope in the*

---

[124] Evelyn Underhill, The Top 80 Evelyn Underhill Quotes (2022 Update), *Quote Fancy*, retrieved from https://quotefancy.com/evelyn-underhill-quotes

future, then there's power in the present to deal with whatever mess you're dealing with in your life, to step through, to hang in there, to persevere, to continue to believe in something, and that's what my relationship with Christ did for me...[125]

God will do that for you and me, as well, amidst tragedy and heartache. Paul wrote:

2 Corinthians 4:8-9, MSG – *We've been surrounded and battered by troubles, but we're not demoralized; we're not sure what to do, we know that God knows what to do; we've been spiritually terrorized, but God hasn't left our side; we've been thrown down, but we haven't broken.*

Imagine. God knows what to do every time. His wisdom is matchless.

"God is our refuge [protects, shields, guards] *and strength* [keeps us strong],[126] *always ready* [very accessible] *to help in times of trouble"* (Psalm 46:1-3, NLT). That's the simple truth, and here are the results and the key to handling life's troubling details.

*So we will not be afraid if the earth should shake
not even if the mountains should fall into the sea;
nor even if the oceans roar and rage
and the hills are violently shaken.*[127]

No fear. No worry. No sleepless nights. No racing thoughts. Just…peace and resting faith in the God Who has got you covered,

---

[125] Zach Lentz, Dabo Swinney's Faith is More Important Than Trophies, *All Clemson Fan Nation/Sports Illustrated*, Jul 16, 2021, retrieved from https://www.si.com/college/clemson/football/dabo-swinneys-faith-is-more-important-than-trophies#:~:text=When%20you%20hoist%20a%20trophy,everything%20else%2C%20not%20just%20football.

[126] Robert G. Bratcher and William Reyburn, *A Handbook on the Book of Psalms*, (United Bible Societies), retrieved from the Logos Bible Software, 2001-2010.

[127] Robert G. Bratcher and William D Reyburn, *A Translator's Handbook On The Book Of Psalms* (United Bible Societies, 1991), 432.

whose *"armies [are] here among us"* (Psalm 46:7, 11, NLT) to ensure that His will is done in my life. The phrase is repeated twice just in case you and I miss the certainty of the sovereignty and authority of God at work in every step we take in this world. Remember Elisha's servant, Gehazi, who panicked and feared for his life, but caught a glimpse of the *"chariots of fire all around,"* heaven's army, paused on a hill, decked out in battle array, and ready to execute God's orders (2 Kings 6:8-23). It is the very reason the psalmist can challenge my weak-knee thinking and knee-jerk reactions when trouble strikes. *"Cease* [imperative] *striving, and know* [again an imperative] *that I am God... The LORD of Heaven's Armies is here among us"* (Psalm 46:7, 10-11, NLT). That's all I truly need to know to put an end to my negative thoughts and disruptive attitudes. Knowing God and His desire for me to live in victory, I am able to surrender to His will and trust the outcomes to Him, regardless of what that may look like.

I found the following prayer in an article entitled, *"When You Have Hard Questions For God,"* by Sarea Geringer. Read it. Focus. And in the end, surrender to the wisdom, goodness, faithfulness, and the unfathomable, mysterious, deep love of God, and then *"trust God from the bottom of your heart"* (Proverbs 3:5, MSG) to carry you through whatever mess and hurt you're dealing with in your life. There is no other place to go but to God when heartbreak and despondency arise.

Heavenly Father,
I praise you as the One Who Knows All.
Nothing is hidden from you.
In your majesty and transcendence,
you hold all the answers.
None of my hard questions drive you away from me.
I confess I have been reluctant to ask you
these hard questions, Lord.
I may not like what you have to say,
and I worry that you won't respond.

Today I trust you to answer in ways that are for my good.
If you withhold or postpone answers,
I trust that you are good.
If you give me answers I didn't expect,
I still trust that you are good.
What's more important than the answers
is my connection with you.
Deepen and strengthen my relationship with you, Jesus.
Thank you for making my approach to the throne possible
through the shedding of your blood on the cross,
and your resurrection power.
Help me recognize the working
of the Holy Spirit in my life.
I surrender my heartache and frustration to you now.
I thank you in advance for the answers you
are preparing to reveal.[128]

Amen!

---

[128] Sarah Geringer, When You Have Hard Questions for God, *Finding Peace in God's Word*, July 15, 2020, retrieved from https://www.sarahgeringer.com/hard-questions-for-god/.

About the Author

Sanford "Sandy" Zensen is an ordained Baptist and former Christian & Missionary Alliance minister with twenty plus years' experience in pastoral ministry. In addition, he has served twenty-five years as a professor of Christian studies and as a Christian college administrator. He holds two professional degrees, MDiv and DMin, and a PhD in religion and society.

Sandy is a frequent speaker at churches, men's ministries, college alumni functions, and athletic events. He was the 2014 AGS (Adult and Graduate Studies) commencement speaker at Bryan College (Tennessee). He is the author of four books, On the Wall with Sword and Trowel: The Challenges and Conflicts of Ministry (WIPF and Stock, 2019), Living Deep in a Shallow World (WIPF and Stock, 2020), The Most Important Decision You'll Ever Make: The Journey to Find and Follow God (WIPF and Stock, 2021), and The Divine Inquiry: Questions Jesus Asked to Change Your Life. He continues to serve as a member and Sunday school teacher at Stuart Heights Baptist Church, one of the largest Southern Baptist churches in the city of Chattanooga, Tennessee.

www.ingramcontent.com/pod-product-compliance
Lightning Source LLC
Chambersburg PA
CBHW071444160426
43195CB00013B/2027